Testimony

The Transformative Power
of Unitarian Universalism

Meg Riley, Editor

Skinner Hou

www.skinnerhouse.org

Printed in the United States

Cover and text design by Suzanne Morgan

print ISBN: 978-1-55896-806-6
eBook ISBN: 978-1-55896-807-3

6 5 4 3 2 1 / 20 19 18 17

Library of Congress Cataloging-in-Publication Data

Names: Riley, Meg, editor.
Title: Testimony : the transformative power of Unitarian Universalism / Meg Riley, editor.
Description: Boston : Skinner House Books, 2017. | Includes bibliographical references.
Identifiers: LCCN 2017023003 (print) | LCCN 2017038617 (ebook) | ISBN 9781558968073 | ISBN 9781558968066 (pbk. : alk. paper)
Subjects: LCSH: Unitarian Universalist Association--Biography. | Unitarian Universalists—-Biography.
Classification: LCC BX9867 (ebook) | LCC BX9867 .T47 2017 (print) | DDC 289.1/320922--dc23
LC record available at https://lccn.loc.gov/2017023003

"Sharing Our Faith" by William G. Sinkford previously appeared in *The Unitarian Universalist Pocket Guide*, Fourth Edition, published by Skinner House Books; "Coming Home" by Kay Montgomery previously appeared in *The Unitarian Universalist Pocket Guide*, Fifth Edition, published by Skinner House Books; "Notes in the Margins" by James C. Key previously appeared in *Humanist Voices in Unitarian Universalism*, published by Skinner House Books; and "Three Ways Unitarian Universalism Has Helped with My Depression" by Kenny Wiley previously appeared in *UU World* magazine on May 9, 2016.

To all those who give and receive precious life from Unitarian Universalism, including those who went before and those who will come after.

And most especially to those who have had to fight to hold onto this faith and to be held onto by this faith.

Your decision to stay makes all the difference.

Contents

Preface	Meg Riley	vii
Saving Our Lives	Roberta Finkelstein	1
Love Without Conditions	Lauren Hulse	5
Heart's Opening	Scott Sammler-Michael	11
A Search for Truth and Meaning	Aneesa Shaikh	21
The Playground Atheist Gets Saved	Jake Morrill	27
Not the Last to Need Saving	Megan Dowdell	33
Sharing Our Faith	William G. Sinkford	37
Home at Last	John Sanger	43
Life-Altering Grace	Manish Mishra-Marzetti	47
Three Ways Unitarian Universalism Has Helped with My Depression	Kenny Wiley	59
Back from Despair	Ted R. Ogg	65
The Unitarian Universalists Believed in My Inherent Worth and Dignity	Mike Smith	69
Ministry with Integrity	Cynthia A. Snavely	75
My Eureka Moment	Tamara Angelique (AKA Thomas E. Flick)	79
I Am a Lotus Flower	Devi Pierce	83
My Friend, the Unitarian Universalist	Phillip Cory Moore	91
Coming Home	Kathleen Montgomery	95

Borderline Child of God	Kelly Murphy Mason	101
Carl Scovel Saved My Life	Roger Butts	117
Emptying My Shoe	Suzi Chase	121
I Am Not Alone	Devalois LeBrón	131
Better Later Than Never	Sharon Peddy Baker	133
The Ultimate Fighting Church	David McBreen	135
Unitarian Universalism Helped Me Find My Awesome	Melanie Christiansen	137
A Perfect Match	Bruce Robinson	143
A Spiritual Journey	Kathy White	149
The Spiritual Sense I Needed	Jack W. Rogers	155
Why I Am a Unitarian Universalist	Leslie T. Grover	157
My Awakening	Karen J. McFarland	165
The Mountain	Eric Bliss	175
A Journey of Faith for Out Lesbians in the Deep South	Nan L. White	179
Most of All, Mindfulness	Israel Luis Sanchez	185
Finding My People and Myself	Marie Luna	187
Saved by the Light	W. Garrett Jackson	191
A Gift to Me	Aisha Hauser	195
Receiving and Giving	James Rogers	199
I Only Have to Be Myself	Mark T. Vogt	205
A Message of Peace and Hope	Eddee Daniel	209
What Church Says That?!	Donald Ernest Allee	217
Notes in the Margins	James C. Key	221
From the Cellblock to Seminary	Eli Poore	229
Together We Know Freedom	Nathan C. Walker	245

Preface

When I was growing up as a Unitarian Universalist kid, my aunt and uncle sent my family a subscription to a magazine called *Guideposts*. My parents rolled their eyes and apparently never gave it a second thought. But I loved it. I would find it tossed carelessly with other discarded mail, and smuggle it immediately to my bedroom to savor.

Guideposts was filled with stories of people in all kinds of trouble, people with woes, whose lives were saved by accepting Jesus Christ as their savior. No problem was too great for Jesus. I was less interested in Jesus, though, than I was in the lurid descriptions of accidental pregnancies, torrid love affairs, bankruptcies, lying, cheating, stealing, and all the other human struggle and strife that preceded the formulaic happy endings.

Internet research tells me that the magazine was founded by Norman Vincent Peale, with the intention of helping people live positive lives. As an adult, I know it's just plain hard to be a human being and live a positive life, and I'm for anything that helps people do it. All of us are vulnerable to illness, loss, and being hurt by people we thought we could trust. All of us do things we wish we hadn't and have things happen to us that aren't our fault. All of us disappoint the people we love and betray our own deepest values sometimes. Some of us suffer in mundane and profound ways because of systems of oppression and violence that were rigged against us long before we were born. Some of us struggle with chronic physical or emotional pain. Life is hard.

That Unitarian Universalist family I was raised in? It was a challenging one. I related to the misery of the writers in *Guideposts* because of the pain in my own home and my own body. I didn't know yet that everyone on the planet was struggling with something. I just knew my life was filled with problems too big to solve, pain with no avenue for healing, a family riddled with terror and rage and violence and silence. I couldn't have named the forces working against my parents, and other families like us, then.

In my own life, healing and transformation have not transpired in one dramatic, tear-filled experience of relinquishment. My own salvation, to the extent that it's useful to talk about personal salvation at all, has been a series of moments that have brought me closer to the person I want to be, in relationships I trust embodying mutual values. Or, as singer-songwriter Ferron wrote, "I'm nobody's savior, and nobody's mine either/ I hear the desert wind whisper, 'But neither are we alone.'"

Truthfully, I have no interest in a faith that isn't saving people. What's the point? I know, though, that this language horrifies some Unitarian Universalists. So when we solicited stories for this anthology, we used a variety of words: How did Unitarian Universalism transform you? Heal you? Change you? Help you? I am hungry for these stories now, as I was hungry for the stories of suffering and redemption as a kid, because every day I forget that healing or redemption is possible. Every day I forget how strong love is. Every day I sink into despair about this precious planet and the greed that is choking out life, and I begin to believe that there is no way forward. Every day I need to know that I'm not alone in my struggle to return to love and to re-center myself in grace and decency. Every day I need to know that I'm part of something much bigger than myself and that, whether or not we can save each other and the planet, my tiny acts of faith matter. So, yes, saying that Unitarian Universalism "saves" people makes many folks uncomfortable. It would make me more uncomfortable if I hadn't seen it happen over and over. And experienced it myself.

I couldn't name the destructive forces at work in my family of origin when I was a child. I did know, however, because I could feel it in my body, that the UU Fellowship was the one place we could go in Charleston, West Virginia, where my parents were happy and relaxed. Where they remembered who they were, and thus allowed their kids to breathe as well.

Is being able to catch someone's eye and laugh, to know that we are with others who care about the same issues of justice and oppression that we do, enough to save people? Is being with others who respect the wisdom of metaphor and poetry enough to save people? Being with others who know there is no one name or story big enough to hold the magnificent complexity of the universe, who are curious to learn more from every source possible—is this enough to save people? I'd say the absence of such companionship is enough to damn people. Think how stifling it feels to be in a room in which everyone there has values that you abhor. You can't connect; if you're there long enough you start to wonder if your own beliefs are wrong. Much of the healing and transformation in the stories you'll read here is grounded in deep companionship, in the writers' learning that they are not alone.

This healing companionship is a matter of faith for Unitarian Universalists. It's the companionship of spiritual ancestors who dreamed of a faith grounded in love for all, a love so great that it would not be eclipsed by any other force. It's the companionship of people all over the world who know the truth of the gathering principles and purposes of Unitarian Universalism. It's the eternal flickering of the chalice flame in the mind's eye. It's the familiarity of favorite bars of music, sung together. It's the companionship of dreamers who dare to imagine acts of justice and compassion and painstakingly seek to create the world we want to live in. It's the fresh air in the room when minds are open to learning and change.

My wish is that each reader finds companionship in this book. The authors are a varied lot—I encourage you to look for stories that inspire you and let go of the rest. I'm delighted to include a number of the members of the Church of the Larger Fellowship who are currently incarcerated. These folks inspire me on a daily basis, living their commitment to our faith in circumstances I can barely imagine.

And may Unitarian Universalism save you, change you, help you, heal you, transform you, one day at a time, in ways that are just right for you!

—Meg Riley

Saving Our Lives

Roberta Finkelstein

This church saves lives. It will save your life if you let it. Not just your life, of course, but all of our lives. I know because years ago this church saved my life.

In 1981, I had finally come back to church after a ten-year absence. I was pregnant with our first child, and my husband Barry and I both felt the need to be connected to a community of faith, for all of the same reasons that many people come to church initially: "for the children." But we hadn't gotten involved at all—just came most Sundays and didn't really know anybody. Just before the baby was due, I signed up to join a women's group, thinking that as a new mom I would need some kind of supportive and adult outlet.

And then the unthinkable happened: the baby was stillborn. Devastated doesn't even begin to describe how we felt on that bleak December day when we arrived to attend the memorial service for our son Brian, a service held in a sanctuary all decked out for Christmas. The minister, Kim Beach, was wonderful—present and supportive and eloquent in reminding our gathered friends and family that we had, in one moment, been bereaved and become parents. I will always be grateful for those words.

Also present that day were some people that I didn't know—members of the women's group that I had not yet attended. They came, they brought food, they introduced themselves to me, assuring me that I was already a member of the group. That group became my lifeline in the following months. They were strangers who became friends, who welcomed me, cried with me, encouraged me, pushed me when I thought about giving up.

My story is a story of pain and loss and gratitude and redemption. The church saved my life. And through this experience I came to understand that the purpose of the church is to save lives.

My story is a story of what happens when we are at our best, not necessarily how we are every minute of every day. But every minute of every day is not a life-saving minute. All I know is that at those times when one of us needs a lifeline, the rest of us are ready to offer it. We may be clumsy, we may miss the mark the first time we throw it. But we will keep trying, and we will gather more people around to help us rather than trying to do it alone. And in the end, we will fulfill our primary function and we will save each other's lives. Over and over again.

The church saved my life. That's how I learned the real reason why the church exists. That's why I'm a minister. Sometimes that gets lost in all the other things that the church does in the meantime, in between life-saving exercises. But all of what we do is in service of readying ourselves for the next life-saving exercise. We have potluck dinners and Salad Sundays and other chances to get together in fellowship, and we have fun and enjoy each other. The board makes policy decisions and keeps an eye on the budget, the council coordinates the yearly calendar, we plan worship services and adult education programs and musical events, we orient and welcome new members, we teach our children. We do all of these things day in and day out. And then somebody gets sick, or loses their job, or finds themselves mourning the death of a loved one. And then, no matter what we were busy doing, we remember that the purpose of this church is to save each other's lives. And we do just that. Over and over again.

I am eternally grateful to have been the beneficiary of the Unitarian Universalist life-saving operation when I most needed it. In those difficult days my life was saved

and the seeds of my ministry were sown. Out of grati-
tude I intend to remain a faithful part of the Unitarian
Universalist life-saving operation for as long as I am able.
I hope you will be there as well.

Love Without Conditions

Lauren Hulse

Two years ago, one morning in the middle of winter, I realized the danger of my situation. I was in a partnership characterized primarily by emotional and physical abuse by a man who was an alcoholic, severely mentally ill, and sometimes violent. I had left my hometown and moved to the other side of the country (to Boise, Idaho) to be with him, in a place where I had no family, no friends, no acquaintances, nothing. From the city of Boise, we moved to a refurbished boxcar-turned-cabin an hour's drive into the country up a winding dirt road, where we had no phone line, no Internet access, and only one neighbor within walking distance. The snow came early that year, falling fast and heavy on the day before Thanksgiving, making that long drive out of the hills even more treacherous.

Amazingly, this had all been just tolerable when it was only me that was in danger, but on that morning in the middle of the winter, I was looking at a positive pregnancy test.

My mom and I had started going to Tennessee Valley Unitarian Universalist Church (TVUUC) after she and my dad divorced when I was six, and we attended off and on throughout my childhood, eventually being joined in the church community by my dad, stepmom, and little brother. TVUUC supported me in many different ways through my childhood. When, in elementary school, I was so ostracized by my peers that I chose not to speak, my religious education teacher welcomed me and made sure I got to build a diorama even though we hadn't attended in weeks. When I was an awkward and socially inept middle school student, there was a place for me on a second-hand sofa in the youth room at church anyway. Even when I was a mildly deviant high school student, frequently grounded as punishment, I was still allowed to go to youth group. That was the first community I found that offered love without conditions, the first place where I was encouraged to take a leadership role, my first introduction to social justice, and the first place where my voice was valued.

As a university student I started working in our church's nursery, and when the position of religious education program assistant became open, it was obvious that I should apply for it. I served the church in that role for three years while I was working on my bachelor's degree, eventually also coordinating our young adults group and finding my place in the leadership of our congregation as a member of the staff.

I met David (not his real name) right before I graduated from university, and within weeks he was living with me. Over the course of a few months, my primary relationships started to fail, and my other housemates moved out. That September, David attempted suicide, and after a weeklong stay in an inpatient psychiatric hospital he announced that for the sake of his mental health he was moving back to Boise, and he needed me to go with him. I told the church and my family abruptly that I was leaving, and October found me driving cross-country, solo, with what belongings I'd managed to keep packed tightly in the back of my car.

I lived in Boise with him for several months, but I made no social contacts except for shallow acquaintances with the people who worked at the restaurant where David had gotten a job making pizza. We went a few times to a United Church of Christ church, because that was closer to how David identified than Unitarian Universalism, but even there I couldn't connect. To David, attending the Unitarian Universalist church was out of the question. Eventually, desperate, I decided I was going to go, whether he allowed it or not.

Just pulling into the parking lot, I felt a wave of peace and safety wash over me—two things I had forgotten how to feel. These are my people, I thought. Even though I hadn't met them yet, I knew they were part of my extended Unitarian Universalist family, and that I would be welcomed and accepted there, no matter what. That single Sunday that I visited, I met a couple, Dan and Aria, who gave me their card. "If you ever need anything," they said. It wasn't a big deal to them; offering to be there for a person new to town was just what you do, they felt. But for me it changed everything; now I had friends.

A few weeks later my car broke down and the shop announced that it couldn't be fixed. I paced the icy sidewalk trying to figure out how I was going to get back to the boxcar that night, much less back and forth to work, or ever afford to buy another car. David was nowhere to be found; we had had a fight days before and he had left. In that moment, something broke up inside me and I sobbed; there was no one to call, nowhere to go, and my prospects were looking bleak.

Then I remembered Dan and Aria and I knew all over again that we are never alone, really. We are always a part of everything, and our Unitarian Universalist family web can catch us even when we've left home and moved to the furthest reaches we can imagine. I called them and they said, "We can come get you, of course!

It's no problem, really. No, really, where are you?" They picked me up in their big burgundy Ford Bronco, and we drove all the way out to the boxcar, all those miles up into the hills, talking the whole way.

It wasn't just that they might have literally saved my life by driving me home that winter night—anyone stranded outside would've frozen—it was that they cared for me. As we drove, Aria asked me questions about my faith, my philosophy, my vision and wisdom, and she listened to what I had to say. "I just love to learn about how other people see the world," she told me. In the short months I had been with David, I had forgotten what it felt like to be listened to, to have my ideas respected, and to be treated with care.

Having my inherent worth recognized and honored by Dan and Aria that day planted the seed that cracked open the morning that I found myself staring at a positive pregnancy test, full of joy and sacredness and fear. I knew I had to leave David, to protect this new life that I was carrying and to protect my own.

Back in my hometown, I returned to TVUUC, where the news of my pregnancy was met with joy and love. My friends threw me a baby shower in the fellowship hall, and the staff of the church, knowing that my bicycle commute was an important part of my life, went in together to buy me a bike trailer to tow the baby. After my son was born, he was welcomed in a child dedication during our Sunday worship service, and afterward my friends and I joked that it was a good thing there were no other babies being dedicated that day, because so many people showed up to support us that we wouldn't have wanted the other babies getting jealous.

I guess you could say Unitarian Universalism saved my life before I even lost it, and it saved my son's life, too. If I hadn't known that I have a faith community where I can belong, no matter where I am geographically or how messy or desperate my life may be, I might not have met Dan and Aria that day and been reminded that I am inherently worthy of safety and happiness. If I hadn't had a faith community that I knew would support me no matter where my path led, I might not have been brave enough to leave David. I know that many women have faith communities where they do not find this kind of acceptance. I know that some women, especially those of us who live here in the South, cannot show up single and pregnant in their faith communities, cannot show up and say "My partner hits me" or "I want to have this baby but I don't know how I'm going to do it." But as a Unitarian Universalist, you can. You can show up messy and hungry and lost and afraid, you can show up with nothing to offer, having made every mistake there is to make, and still be met with forgiveness and acceptance and love without conditions.

Heart's Opening

Scott Sammler-Michael

Before seminary I worked as an electrician out of IBEW local 24, in Baltimore. I first realized that I was called to ministry on a jobsite: the Mustard Gas Neutralization Facility at Edgewood Arsenal. Really. Near the entrance gate, next to the time clock, someone had placed a big arrow pointing down at a trashcan. Above the arrow, a sign demanded, "Leave your feelings HERE." This was an unusually blatant display of a golden rule of the macho world of industrial construction: "Your whole self is not welcome here." Now, there is some logic to discouraging emotional outbursts on construction sites. There's a job to be done, and it requires focus and precision. Especially in the electrical trade, a lack of focus can result in—well, fire and death.

The construction site is not the only place our whole selves are not welcome. Public displays of emotion are discouraged, and they make others uncomfortable. Our culture prefers us to keep our feelings to ourselves, especially when one of those feelings is sorrow. But the injunction to "leave your feelings at the gate" is repressive and corrosive. We are taught that this emotionless half-self is the only self of worth and dignity.

We need places where we can be our whole selves, and communities that will hold us as we cry, smile as we rejoice, and nurture us as we connect the disparate pieces of ourselves that have been scattered by the cacophony of modern life.

A study published in the *American Sociological Review* in 2006 compared the intimacy of social networks in 1985 and in 2004. In 1985, the most common answer to the question "In how many people do you confide?" was "Three." In 2004, the most common answer was "Zero." Nearly 25 percent of survey respondents said there was *no one* in their lives to whom they could express their true selves.

A deep-seated isolation lurks in the hearts and lives of many Americans, and its consequences are myriad. Isolation begets loneliness. It obscures our inherent interdependence. Isolation causes stress and shortens lives. It makes us believe our options are limited. This survey reveals an opportunity for congregations to embrace an essential mission: to assuage isolation by cultivating genuine human connection. Nurturing souls with the gift of human contact is a powerful form of social action. People long to express their deepest yearnings and to be held with love as they do so.

Sometimes we can feel isolated even in the midst of a mighty crowd. The project I was working on at the Mustard Gas Neutralization Facility was mandated by the international Chemical Weapons Convention, and it had nearly four hundred employees. Yet there were times I felt completely alone. I was the control wire foreman for Building 4, and it is true that a foreman is not always "one of the men." A good foreman inspires, motivates, and rewards, yes, but also needs a sense of detachment. Foremen have to lay people off—not because they are not good workers, but because the need for workers fluctuates over the course of a project. When one phase ends and the next is not yet ready to begin, "reduction in force" layoffs come around, usually according to seniority.

As a foreman, I kept my distance in many ways. By reading. By eating lunch alone. By poring over plans. The "tough-guy" culture of the jobsite means that those in charge are especially forbidden to express much emotion except occasional anger, some laughter (sadly, often at inappropriate practical jokes), and the necessary "attaboy!" for a job well done.

And then one day a man we called "Squiggy" sat down at the lunch table where I was reading. Construction workers often have nicknames; I never knew his real name. Squiggy was the king of the over-the-top practical jokes, and at first I assumed he was messing with me. But when I looked up, his eyes were filled with tears. I put down my book, and he opened up to me, as if I were his chaplain. He shared that his girlfriend was cheating on him and running up his credit cards. He was very afraid that the other men would see him sharing his despair, so I took him into the foreman's trailer where he could hide. Here he was, a strong, seasoned wireman, on a job with men who had been his colleagues for twenty years, on a jobsite with four hundred men, and he chose to confide in me, someone he had known for less than two months. He was in isolation. And he showed me I was a chaplain, a minister. He saw it before I did.

Like Squiggy, all of us too often find ourselves isolated and our emotions locked up. In American culture, girls are told never to be angry, and boys never to be sad or tender. When I was in high school in the late 1970s, someone wrote lines from sappy popular songs all over my desk: lines like "You know it's you, babe" and "You're once, twice, three times a lady." One day I arrived in class early and caught the scribbler in the act. It was Steve, a big tough kid, a linebacker and a ruffian. The lyrics he wrote on the desk were silly love songs. They were expressions of emotions his social circles denied. Music was the vehicle that gave him permission to express his tenderness, but it lived only on that desk, hidden.

Music did the same for me. As a youth I often sat alone in my room, listening to pop music and crying—crying for love, loss, the state of the world, my own confusion about human relationships. Like Steve's, my feelings remained private. Though they longed, needed, to be shared, my tenderest emotions lived only in isolation. This may explain why ironworkers, welders, plumbers, and electricians love sappy country songs, and why they play them so loudly at work. It's how they bring their feelings—their whole selves—past the gate.

We all need to be able to feel deeply and express our truth freely. Religious communities are powerful venues for evoking and enabling that emotional freedom, pulling us out of isolation. Reverent attention to the holy helps us feel complete, safe, worthy. Church helped me express my whole self in public, with liberty and power. In May 2003, while I was still foreman on that jobsite, members of my fellowship and I attended Union Sunday at the First Unitarian Church of Baltimore. This is the annual celebration of Channing's famous sermon "Unitarian Christianity," delivered in Baltimore in 1819, and my friends and I wanted to celebrate our faith tradition in that beautiful old church. That Sunday, Rev. Rob Hardies preached a sermon titled "Religion Is for Lovers." Hardies proclaimed, "Religion is for lovers: lovers of truth, lovers of justice, lovers of our full humanity." As I heard those words, the door to my heart opened wide. I started to nod, and sob, and then shake, trembling with tears. I was not alone. That day I realized that Unitarian Universalism granted me license to be completely human—that it encouraged my whole self to enter the room and shine forth in the company of folks covenanted to worship together and to hold one another. It countermanded the jobsite injunction against my emotional self. I had grown up a Southern Baptist, and this release felt like salvation, like being born again.

Healthy religious communities nurture the dignity of the whole human person, walking with us through whatever darkness may descend. Unitarian Universalism gives my blue-collar male self the permission to proclaim, "I am holy; I feel, therefore I am human." It rewards me for truly feeling and expressing the emotions that define my core.

We are not really taught how to embrace or manage our emotions. Emotions take longer to process than words or problems or ideas, and we process them with everything that we are and everything that we do: with our bodies, memory, and appetite; in sleep, exercise, lovemaking, being alone, being in public . . . whatever it is we need in those holy moments.

Our culture's emotional cluelessness can make us miss the holiest message of all: that true love is boundless. Human beings have ways of thwarting and twisting love, but divine love—divine love knows no limits. This is the core of Universalism. My love has limits, and yours might, too; but divine love, that which loved everything into existence and the promise of well-being—is *limitless*. This is what Jesus means when he says, "The Kingdom is come"—he doesn't say the Kingdom *will* come. Using the present tense, he teaches that it is upon us now, so "let all with eyes to see and ears to hear understand." The kingdom, our spiritual need to be whole, and the beauty of our inner grace—all of that lies *here*—*now*—awaiting our awakening, craving our embrace. The transcendent longs for us to extravagantly celebrate the fact that we are worthy of love because we have sparks of divinity sewn into the fabric of our souls; our heart smiles at the hope of a peaceful, loving world, even when it may seem unattainable.

Too many people never grant themselves permission to experience their emotions in all their rich fullness. Because I am a white, educated, urban, straight man from blue-collar roots, leaving my feelings at the gate was the price I paid to earn a living. Yes, there is too much sexism and misogyny in our culture, but we ask terrible things of men: "Don't cry. Toughen up." Maybe this is why men are often unlikely to speak easily of spiritual and emotional things. But I'll tell you a secret—a giddy, awesome, sweet little secret: I was unable to discover my spiritual grounding and a deeper, manly strength until I gave myself permission to feel deeply. My image of the divine and how I partook of it came clear only after I allowed myself to mourn the death of love, to cry at senseless destruction, to feel at one with the oppressed, to shout with rage at injustice and terror, within a community of folks who cared for and held me. Only then did the pieces of my scattered humanity coalesce and form a newer, better, more powerful man.

Our humanity, our divinity, our salvation lies in how we say yes to the gifts and beauty offered us. And if we say yes and commit to love, our blinders fall away, and love is restored. Faith is at its core faith in love: love of self, of life, of relationship. It is an acknowledgment that we are lovable. In this embrace we write new stories of ourselves as beings created by and for love.

I know that Unitarian Universalism saves lives, because it saved mine. Salvation is no metaphor. Unitarian Universalism offers us a faith that restores vision, a faith that is emotionally literate, intellectually mature, socially relevant, spiritually grounded, morally courageous, ethically innovative, concerned for others, and self-loving—especially when things fall apart. Our focus on the transformative power of love derives from the intuition that we are expressions of divinity in the deepest core of our souls. And because of this we are called to unconditional, redemptive love. We love ourselves by loving each other by loving ourselves by loving each other—and in doing so we imitate the divine, that creative power of the universe and of human culture, the only way we can: with our whole beings.

This reminds me of John Lennon singing, "Whatever gets you through the night, it's all right, it's all right." Whatever it takes for us to feel completely human, for us to get through the night, to recall that the fabric of our being is love, is all right. Our whole selves need to be nurtured and coaxed into connection. Try as we may, we can never leave our feelings at the gate.

A Search for Truth and Meaning

Aneesa Shaikh

I discovered Unitarian Universalism at around age thirteen, after a long and unsatisfying search for a spiritual community that matched what I felt I needed. I was newly separated from the faith I was born into and had never been more confused about what I believed.

My parents met in college at Baylor University in Texas, my mom a first-generation college student from a very poor Missouri family and my dad a first-generation immigrant who had just arrived in the United States after growing up in India and spending a few years in Nigeria. They were an unlikely match. My mom was raised Southern Baptist and my dad Muslim, further adding to their differences. When they got engaged, my mom converted to Islam so she could marry my dad. My mom had always been a religious woman and found herself quite liking the community that came with the Muslim faith, and once my

sister and I were born, it seemed a given that we would
be raised as Muslims. And so we were, and I have many
a fond memory of Ramadans, Eids, and Jum'ahs from the
first thirteen years of my life. I never really had any problems with the principles of the faith or their manifestation
in my life, and in fact felt very connected to the five pillars
of Islam and was proud of my faith.

But at some point shortly after my maternal grandmother passed away, I started to question whether or not
I believed in God, and knew I needed to look within a
bit more. I slowly started to accept that the belief in God
was so central to Islam that I didn't feel I could continue
to practice it anymore. I told my father, who was understandably upset to hear his thirteen-year-old daughter
make such a decision. Things were awkward between us
for a short while, but at some point he came to me with
words I'll never forget: "Aneesa, I realize that in this situation, I can either be angry that my daughter has made
a choice I likely won't be able to change, or I can be
proud that I've raised a daughter strong enough to think
for herself and make her own choices." Both my parents
ended up supporting me in this journey, and I am eternally grateful for their willingness to let me search freely
and responsibly for truth and meaning.

So began my journey to find something that suited
me better. I went with a friend to her synagogue, but

didn't quite find what I was looking for. I went to different churches with a few other friends, but couldn't quite get behind that either. I read about Buddhism, the Bahá'í faith, United Methodism, and almost everything in between. But nothing felt right.

One day, while surfing the web in a last ditch effort to find something I felt connected to, I haphazardly Googled "liberal faith community Bellevue, WA" and stumbled upon a blog post that someone had written about Unitarian Universalism. The author of the post was reflecting on their first experience at a Unitarian Universalist congregation and their description of the community seemed like exactly what I'd been looking for. I found a UU church just a few minutes from my home and decided to check it out the next Sunday. One of my parents dropped me off, and I went in by myself. I was greeted immediately by a somewhat confused-looking member of the congregation who was wondering who I was and why I was there all alone. She asked me what I was looking for, and I said, fully expecting to be met with a weird look, "Well, I'm kind of Muslim, kind of Atheist, and really confused, so . . . I guess I don't really know what I'm looking for." To my complete surprise, she put her arm around me, smiled, led me into the sanctuary, and said, "I think this is just the place for you."

It was, indeed, just the place for me. I kept going back every week after that, and eventually roped my sister into joining me. She liked it, too, so we started going together, and at some point my mom joined us. One Sunday, timidly, my dad joined us as well, and found himself enjoying it. Within about a year, the whole family was going, and I think it was a really good thing for us. We still keep Islam very close to our hearts, and it will always be a part of our mixed-up, complex family culture. But we are all very different people, and Unitarian Universalism gave us the freedom we all needed to develop our deeper beliefs and figure out what worked for us as individuals. It significantly changed the way I live my life. It made me more mindful and reflective, taught me to think more inclusively about the big picture, and opened doors to opportunities I may never otherwise have had access to.

One of these was the UUA's Youth and Young Adults of Color Multicultural Leadership School, which taught me invaluable information about cross-cultural leadership and opened my eyes to several new aspects of my own identity. I got to co-lead a workshop at General Assembly in Providence, have given several mini-sermons, and have a huge, incredible network of friends, mentors, and teachers within the UU community. I have also been forced to confront the reality that no institution is exempt from institutionalized systems of oppression. It was disillusioning at first to realize that even within something as seemingly perfect as Unitarian Universalism, white supremacy and other oppressive structures are not only present but prevalent. But this understanding has enabled me to more holistically work toward justice and liberation in all aspects of my life.

I wear a chalice necklace every day to center me and remind myself of what is important. I think often about how different my life would have been had I not discovered Unitarian Universalism, and I always find myself thinking that I would be nowhere near the kind of person I am today if not for the decision to keep searching until I found what felt right. Unitarian Universalism has truly changed my life and continues to do so—it challenges me, frustrates me, teaches me, informs me, calms me, and transforms me in ways I never expected.

The Playground Atheist Gets Saved

Jake Morrill

It may be that every elementary school, across the whole South, has at least one self-appointed Playground Atheist. You know the type: When all the other kids are showing off their new WWJD bracelets and mooning about how cool the youth pastor is, there's a sharp-eyed fellow, standing there by the slide, not believing any of it for a second. When the typical debates come up—for instance, whether dogs go to heaven—it's the Playground Atheist who explodes the whole conversation. "Heaven!" he'll say. "Heaven?! What are you, a moron?" Yes, it's this kind of gentle, persuasive approach that has endeared Playground Atheists to junior Christians through the Southland for time immemorial. And, at Bearden Elementary School, as the Reagan years came into full bloom, the Playground Atheist was me.

From time to time, the Tennessee State Legislature will cook up a wild idea. So it happened, when I was in fourth grade, that a reporter from the local NBC affiliate came to visit, with a cameraman in tow. The legislators in Nashville were considering whether to mandate prayer in school, and this reporter was on a mission to find out what the fourth-graders thought.

To start off, she had us all bow our heads, our hands folded on our desks. Then, she opened it up for discussion. Well, what did we think? To absolutely no one's surprise, it was Matthew who spoke first. Everyone in the zip code knew Matthew loved Jesus. Just adored him. Brought him up all the time. So, his eyes shining, Matthew accepted the chance to lay out his convictions. All around the room, heads were nodding. The reporter gave thanks, then asked if there were others. A girl in the back chimed in, to reinforce Matthew's point: this was a world that stood ever in need of more prayer.

Reporters are trained to fish for intrigue, for friction. So, as hands waved in the air, she wondered if anyone had a different opinion. The hands dropped. There was silence. A friend is someone who knows just what lapses in judgment you are prone to make, and will leap in to stop you. My lapses tend to involve talking at times when I shouldn't. I recall my good friend Jeff, in those slow-motion seconds, staring at me intently from across the room, shaking his head, and mouthing the word "Don't." But there it was. I had raised my hand. The microphone dangled close. The camera drew near. The room emptied of air.

Later, I recalled having mentioned things I happened to know about the Constitution. I still believe it is possible I uttered the phrase "church and state." But none of these high-minded words and ideals appeared on the local news that evening at 6:00 and 11:00, and again on the early-morning show. No, instead, what the good people of East Tennessee saw was a chubby boy with thick glasses announcing to the whole world that God didn't exist.

As soon as the reporter departed, the whisper of scandal began threading its way through the entire fourth grade. And then the whole school. By the next morning, certain classmates were able to tell me just what their parents thought about a boy who'd say something like that on TV. My parents, I gather, also received some feedback. What I had was not fame. It was outright infamy. Before, my atheism had been an occasional source of wonder to others. They felt the kind of pride you feel when a neighbor happens to own an exotic bird of bright plumage; it was a thrill to be in proximity to something so odd. The Christians even seemed to enjoy my earnest challenges, seeing them perhaps as a kind of a trial. But this time, it seemed, the Playground Atheist had taken it too far. To say something hateful about Jesus at recess was one thing. To broadcast it so everyone could hear it? Unacceptable.

The week dragged on, as I found myself shunned by my classmates. But then, on Thursday afternoon, two handwritten letters arrived, both from the Tennessee Valley Unitarian Universalist church. One was from my Sunday School teacher; the other from the minister of religious education. Without even opening the envelopes, I knew what to expect. And sure enough, there it was: They were proud. Not of my atheism, per se. But of the character they said they saw in what I'd done. Like the ancient prophets our Sunday School class was studying that year, said one, I had stood my ground and had said what I thought. The next day, the purgatory of exclusion continued. But somehow, I didn't mind it as much—a cold shoulder was nothing beside what Jonah or Amos had faced. And by Monday, it seemed, all was back to normal.

In the years since, my theology has evolved. I have taken Communion, stopped in awe before mountains. I have prayed till tears came, and sat in meditation for long hours in a dark Buddhist Zendo. But, truth be told, it was as an atheist that I first came to see, in a way that was real and has not failed me since, how I am part of a love wider than my own life, and how that spacious embrace makes itself known to me, most often, through a community like the one that first told me, "You are not alone."

Not the Last to Need Saving

Megan Dowdell

When I was eleven years old, I entered a New England
Unitarian Universalist church for the first time on my
own. I was invited to sing in the youth choir that traveled among several churches downtown. After one
session in the religious education program, I wanted
to return every week. Arriving without my parents, I
quickly became an adopted child of the church. A family
would bring me along to the church retreat and make
sure I had a ride to come serve food at the silent auction
or volunteer in the childcare program. Looking back,
I wonder what the members must have thought about
this young girl who was always the first to arrive and the
last to leave. Of course, what they didn't know then was
that my home was not a safe place. I suffered consistent
abuse by my father and experienced prolonged periods
of silence and neglect. Some might call this *hell*. The

weekends, when school was not in session, were the most dangerous times in the week. If there was a task at church I was allowed to do, I would volunteer to be there. If there was any community event or speaker, I would beg to go. My church family truly meant safety and survival at the most vulnerable times.

Just like many fellow victims of trauma and abuse, as a child I believed I had done something to deserve the harm at home. While I remember having dreams of somewhere-else-than-here, I did not imagine a future for myself, or even that my life would extend into adulthood. I do not believe it is an exaggeration to say that I would not have made it through high school without Unitarian Universalism. I am grateful to have stepped into a tradition that rejects the idea of original sin: where we believe that every child is beautiful and every person is worthy of love and nurturing. I was saved by community. I was saved by love. I was saved by faith.

Relationship and trust-building are the foundation of my experience of salvation by Unitarian Universalism. At the church, I had many positive adult role models who offered appropriate friendship and opportunities to play, learn, and lead. When I was sixteen and beginning the process of coming out as queer, the adult leaders offered me the opportunity to co-chair the Welcoming Congregation task force. The church confirmed for me in repeated ways what God already knew: not only was I worthy of love, but I had love to give.

When my brother died on Christmas Day in 1999, it was the director of religious education who picked me up and brought me to her house for the holiday dinner. When I was seventeen, my mother went to apply for a restraining order one Sunday morning, so the youth group advisor picked me up and brought me to the Sunday service. The other single mothers in the church became our network of social support.

And it was the minister who convinced me to get "real help" for the stuff I'd be carrying with me from an abusive childhood. "Don't wait until you're thirty and this all creeps up on you." I can still hear her candid voice and see her raised brow, as I sunk into the couch in the minister's study. Now, at thirty-two, I know that I was saved by her respectful challenge in a community that was worthy of my youthful trust, in a loving tradition that values salvation as human wholeness and health for the long haul of this life. She invited me into another part of Unitarian Universalist salvation: a journey away from being consumed by hate or vengeance, and toward growth, understanding, and even forgiveness. She didn't ask me to erase or forget traumas that had consumed me, but to do the spiritual grief work to forgive myself. Through Unitarian Universalism, I grew into a vision of family and community that condemns violence of all kinds and releases the desire for retribution that would keep me farther from my own flourishing and well-being.

As a Unitarian Universalist, I cannot claim a God who simply damns those who do bad things to hell. Instead I find myself saved in a community that wishes to build a world of justice, mercy, and compassion for all, knowing I am not the last to need saving.

Sharing Our Faith

William G. Sinkford

I found Unitarian Universalism after experiencing other faith communities in my search for a religious home.

I walked into my first Unitarian Universalist congregation at the age of fourteen, almost forty years ago. To say that I had been searching for a religious home would give me far more credit than I deserve. The reality was that I had been accompanying my mother as she searched for a religious home for both of us. And I must acknowledge that I was not always enthusiastic about this search. Churches hadn't been very comfortable places for me, let alone supportive religious homes.

My nuclear family had been unchurched throughout my early years. We are African-American and had attended the Black Episcopal Church in Detroit, Michigan, and the Black Southern Baptist Church in North

Carolina. Even at fourteen, I knew that I did not fit in either church.

The Black Southern Baptist Church in the small North Carolina town where my mother had been reared was the life of the Black community. Everyone knew they were welcome there. But in addition to this sense of acceptance and the joyful song and prayer life, "hellfire" was preached from the pulpit. Somehow I could not believe in a God who would damn some people to hell.

The Black Episcopal Church in Detroit was light on hellfire, but heavy on the liturgical mysteries of transubstantiation and the strange (to me) concept of the triune God. This upper middle-class congregation seemed far more concerned with the labels in my clothes and the type of car we drove than with the state of my soul, let alone with my theological struggles.

By age fourteen I had decided that Christianity was not for me. As I look back, I understand that my age at the time was at least as important as my theological journey. I took considerable pleasure in the consternation of family and friends when I proclaimed a "stand-up" atheism, savoring their predictable shocked reaction and welcoming the debate that was sure to follow.

My family tried several other mainline Protestant churches and a Baha'i community, but it was not until we walked into First Unitarian in Cincinnati, Ohio, that I found my religious home. Most of the faces in the congregation were white, but many African Americans also were present. The congregation had been very active in the struggle to dismantle segregation in that border town, and African Americans had been drawn to the church and were welcomed as members. The religious educator, Pauline Warfield Lewis, who guided me to the youth group that night, was African-American. I didn't take any polls, of course; I don't know if 10 percent or 20 percent of the congregation were Black, but there were enough persons of color that I knew it was okay to be Black and to be in the presence of whites.

No hellfire was preached from the pulpit. A personal search for meaning and a commitment to justice were the messages. Even my aggressive atheism was acceptable. Not everyone I talked to agreed with me—far from it—but people wanted to hear what was in my heart. I was engaged less in debate and more in conversation in which sharing was possible, perhaps even expected.

I felt wanted and valued by this congregation. "Would you like to join the youth group?" "We're hosting a conference this weekend, can you come?" "Would you help with a worship service?" This was a place where I could bring my whole person.

As a minister now, I sometimes interpret my experience in theological terms: The inherent worth and dignity of every person. Commitment to justice, equity, and compassion. The value of personal story as the basis for theological reflection and religious life. The need to make our congregations places where people do not need to check their identities at the door. The extraordinary experience of covenanted community, committed to living out religious values in the world.

But the reality of my experience has been both less lofty and more profound. The First Unitarian Church in Cincinnati truly welcomed me. The members of the congregation offered themselves in ways that gave me the gift of myself. The standard they embodied was not merely tolerance, but affirmation. I hope and trust that you have had a similar experience in finding your Unitarian Universalist congregation. This faith can be your home.

Since age fourteen, I have had many opportunities to talk about Unitarian Universalism. I have talked to people looking for a new church home and people who have recently moved and become my neighbors. I have chatted with other parents on the sidelines of soccer games or swim meets, sharing bits of personal or family stress. Sometimes in social gatherings it's gratifying to talk about my church and to hear friends say how important the church sounds in my life.

But sometimes, unbidden and as if by an act of grace, a conversation will happen in which the good news of Unitarian Universalism offers hope to someone in need. A few years ago I was riding with another minister in a cab in New York City, on the way to a meeting at one of our congregations. The driver was a recent Haitian immigrant who was, I think, practicing his American English on his passengers.

"What is your business?" he asked. After we told him we were Unitarian Universalist ministers, he asked how our church felt about gay and lesbian people. We answered with our clear affirmation that all people are children of God, that gay and lesbian folks are welcomed in our congregations and in our ministry.

The cabby was silent for a moment and then told the story of his brother, a gay man who had been forced out of his religious home when he was outed in his congregation. "Unitarian Universalist, you say? I wonder if he has heard about your church. I'm glad I have. We need to find a church where we can be together as a family."

I don't know whether this man and his family sought out a Unitarian Universalist congregation. We did suggest a few for him to visit, but I believe that he just needed to know there was at least one church where his family could be together as who they really are.

Our Unitarian Universalist tradition and worshipping communities can help people heal their wounds, build their confidence, find opportunities for self-forgiveness, and restore their self-worth. We need never doubt the value of what we have to offer. May you find your religious home as I have.

Home at Last

John Sanger

There's a Zen saying that has proved itself true for me numerous times: *When the student is ready, the teacher will appear.*

Once, the "teacher" wasn't a person but an organization—the Church of the Larger Fellowship—and it appeared about fifteen years ago. But that's closer to the end of the story than to the beginning, so let's back up about half a century and start this story there.

In the beginning, that is, in my beginning, and throughout the early years of my life, I didn't know anyone who was a Unitarian Universalist. One of my aunts once made a comment about a woman in her circle of acquaintances. "She's a Unitarian," she said, as if it were akin to being a leper. She was of a conservative Christian bent, as were most members of my immediate and extended family.

I assumed everyone was like my family. As I grew older, I found that I was wrong. I began to see some of the differences in people when I left home, joined the U.S. Marines, and went to Vietnam for thirteen months. Those experiences and, after leaving the Marines, the time I spent in college began opening my eyes to the spiritual world around me. Even then, UUs didn't come into my consciousness. The student still wasn't ready.

It wasn't until I crossed the half-century mark—and found myself in prison—that Unitarian Universalism came into my life. And that happened because after nearly five decades of trying to understand evangelical Christianity, I just gave up.

Not long after I came to prison, I met Connor, my first real-life Unitarian Universalist, and we became friends. The more we talked, the more I liked what he had to say about his spiritual path and the principles of Unitarian Universalism. He gave me a copy of *UU World*. I liked what I read there. A lot.

Shortly after meeting Connor, I met a UU minister. She had traveled all the way across the state to attend a three-day interfaith event organized by several inmates. I was impressed not only that she would travel for hours to come to talk to a bunch of inmates, many of whom felt discarded by the public at large, but also that, well . . . that she was a she. In the only religious training that I'd had as a young person, ministers were men. Only men. Period. Don't ask questions.

I also was impressed by the message she brought to an almost-full auditorium and, later, when we had break-out groups for more intimate conversations. That was my beginning on a path that has led me places I'd never previously imagined. Unitarian Universalism opened new vistas and gave me a new perspective on the term *spiritual path*. That is, it helped me understand a fuller meaning of Antonio Machado's statement, "Traveler, there is no path. Paths are made by walking."

Walking. Doing. Putting thoughts and ideas and beliefs and words into action.

I believe that there are no coincidences or accidents in the universe. Meeting Connor was no accident. Nor was meeting the UU minister. And, not long after that, being introduced to the Church of the Larger Fellowship. It was what I needed at that particular time because I was ready for a teacher. What I now understand: For the first fifty years of my life, I was not ready to appreciate the meaning and the beauty of UU covenants and practices.

I've always been a Unitarian Universalist in spirit and by how I've conducted my life. I just didn't know it until now. When the Church of the Larger Fellowship came into my life and I started meeting UUs, I immediately felt that I had a *home*. And I love that feeling.

Life-Altering Grace

Valentine's Day, 1992. It was my junior year at George-
town University, I was twenty years old, and I was
standing in the middle of Key Bridge, which straddles the
Potomac River between Washington, D.C., and Virginia,
on a day dedicated to romantic love. My life was a mess,
and I figured that I might as well end it. I had grown up
in a traditional Hindu immigrant family, with unambigu-
ous expectations of heterosexual marriage. And I was gay.
I had pretended I wasn't gay. I had tried not to be gay. I
had prayed not to be gay. None of that had worked, and
so here I was: damned if I came out of the closet, with
the possible loss of family, friends, and life as I knew it,
and damned if I didn't, with the inevitability of a straight
marriage that I knew I wouldn't be able to maintain.

As fate would have it, I didn't have a pen or paper
with me at that moment on the bridge, and I could not

fathom ending my life without writing a note that would guilt-trip the world. So I returned to my dorm room, intending to write a note and return to finish the deed. However, once back at school, in a moment of lucidity and desperation I called a classmate, who came over and spent several hours with me. His advice that night, in a nutshell: "If you're going to kill yourself anyway, you might as well try being gay for a while. The bridge isn't going anywhere." The most insane logic can make complete sense at just the right moment! He reached me in my fog, and nudged me in a better direction.

I did want to live, and coming out, for me, proved to be an act of both survival and personal integrity. It also resulted in a simultaneous decision that I would be "spiritual but not religious." I could not find any Hindu communities that might welcome and affirm gay people, and I knew full well how embattled the broader American political and religious landscape was around gay rights. Thus, I reckoned, my spiritual self would be something that I would cultivate on my own, outside of religious structures. I would live the best life that I could, nurturing my own spiritual path, without allowing anyone else's moral judgment to hang over me.

In the early 1990s, with the majority of mainstream religious institutions scornful of gay and lesbian individuals and our relationships, this decision to be "spiritual but not religious" made sense. It was how many, if not most, of my gay friends were responding to religion. However, I had not carefully thought through or deeply explored it. I had assumed that this was my only way forward as an openly gay man. Over time, this decision came to have consequences that I didn't foresee.

On a Friday in August 1998, I had the privilege of attending the wedding of a Hindu-American friend in Maryland. I remember that night in vivid detail. I was so thrilled to reconnect with my friend, under such joyous circumstances, and to attend the event with the man I had been with for five years. My friend's family had overlooked no detail in crafting a wonderful, typically Hindu wedding ceremony for her. The groom arrived at the Marriott hotel where the ceremony was held astride an ornately decorated horse, a very traditional formality that I had only ever seen in India! Inside, hundreds of friends, family members, and guests had turned up from all across the country and even the world to honor the couple. The ceremony was a deeply moving celebration of their love and commitment to one another. As I absorbed the beauty of it all, my tears just flowed and flowed. They continued flowing during the car ride home later that night.

My partner was perplexed, and inquired how I was doing. Through the tears, all I could stammer was, "It was just so beautiful . . . all the family and friends, the religious community that turned up to celebrate her marriage. . . . I just don't know . . . where would we ever get married? Who would come? Who would officiate . . . not just a wedding, but what about when we die? Would any community show up for us . . . would any community care?"

My friend's gorgeous Hindu wedding brought alive for me, in such a stark, painful way, the reality that my "spiritual but not religious" path had ended up a loner path, a path devoid of spiritual community. Yes, I had a community of friends . . . but what I had seen and experienced that evening was different: it was a community of like-minded, like-valued individuals, grounded in ancient traditions, rituals, and symbols, coming together to honor and celebrate one of their own. I didn't have anything like this in my life, and I had never made a deliberate choice not to. Because of the open scorn of so many religious denominations, I had just assumed that I had no options. I feared that my partner and I would never have what I had just witnessed, and I was inconsolable.

The feeling of sadness settled in and deepened overnight. I was working as a diplomat in the U.S. Foreign Service and had recently returned to the U.S. from an assignment in Finland, and I was also missing my friends in Helsinki. So the next morning, a Saturday, I did the logical thing—I placed an international call to Helsinki (in the days before Skype!), to talk with my atheistic Finnish best friend. If anyone could talk me out of this spirituality-induced funk, I knew that a card-carrying atheist could probably do it.

The conversation did not unfold as expected. I got him on the line (at who knows what exorbitant cost per minute!) and spent a good long time bawling, describing to him how lovely the wedding had been, and how spiritually lonely and isolated attending it had made me feel. When I finally let him get a word in edgewise, he said, "Well, you know, wanting community is not a bad thing, and not every community hates gay people." (There was a slight pause before he continued. . . . I sensed just a moment's hesitation.) "Have you heard of the Unitarians?" he asked.

"Who?" I responded.

"Well," he continued, "I don't know that much about them, but we have a small group in Helsinki with about twenty people in it, and they call themselves Unitarian Universalists. I've met one or two of them, they're nice. They follow an ethical path, or something like that."

"Okay, okay," I said, "I'm right near a computer." (Imagine here a bulky old computer with a wired Internet connection.) I waited for my PC to boot up,

even as my phone bill mounted. After several minutes,
I began searching. "How do you spell that? What was
that name you said?" I asked the non-native English
speaker. Patiently, he stayed on the phone with me as the
website of the Unitarian Universalist Association loaded.
I clicked a tab that said "What We Believe" and began
reading the seven Principles out loud. When I finished,
I exclaimed, "*No way!* There can't be a religion that
only believes these things—and they 'value and respect'
wisdom from all the world traditions? They've got to be
a cult! They must ask people to sign their houses over,
once they get them in the door. There are a lot of religions like that. Do you know anything else about them?"

"Well, no," he said; "like I said, we only have twenty
of them in all of Finland. But maybe you can visit one of
their communities and see for yourself."

Yeah, I thought; there probably isn't even one of
these Unitarian Universalist congregations near me. I
went to the "Find a Congregation" tab and entered our
Washington zip code: 20009. At the top of the search
results popped up "All Souls Church, Unitarian, Har-
vard and 15th Streets NW, Washington, D.C. 20009."
The address was just a handful of blocks from where we
lived, practically walking distance. This vague possibility
was now becoming weirdly real. "Should I go?" I wondered. I sure as heck wasn't going to go by myself! That

meant convincing my partner to go with me . . . except that he was an atheistic professor of the sciences. Selling him on organized religion was not going to be easy.

I got off the phone with my best friend in Finland, thanking him and promising to report back. Then I began talking with my partner about attending church the next day. In talking through the possibility with him, I was clear that any community that didn't accept us for who we were—openly gay men in a committed relationship—was not going to work for me. I also wasn't going to "convert" to anything, and so respect for my Hindu heritage was important. For my partner, an atheist and as a scientist, a spiritual experience without a reliance on the supernatural was important; as he put it, "Any 'mumbo jumbo' and I'm outta there!" In this way we agreed on our bottom lines and decided to attend All Souls Church the very next day.

I was scared witless as we entered the church that Sunday morning. The butterflies and gastrointestinal gymnastics roiling my gut were on a par with what one might experience before a really important job interview. In retrospect, I recognize that my physical state was an indication of how much what we were doing mattered to me. I wanted it to "work," whatever that might mean, and I was incredibly afraid that it wasn't going to. What we didn't know that morning was that we were arriving, as complete newbies, in a congregation that had just a few months earlier dismissed its senior minister. With the difficulties surrounding that, many people had left the congregation, and many of those who remained were still navigating feelings of loss and demoralization. We knew none of this, stepping into the community bright-eyed, chipper, and nervous as all heck that morning. (We realized, months later, that we could probably have felt the collective sense of heaviness, if only we hadn't been so wrapped up in our own worries and fears.)

We didn't know where to sit, so we moved up toward the front of the worship space—the seats not often taken. It was only after we had settled in that I noticed the number of older folk around us. My default assumptions about older Americans kicked in, and I immediately began fretting about what it meant for us as a gay couple to be surrounded by all these elders. "If they knew who we are, that we're a couple, they would want us to leave their community," I thought.

All Souls, back then, had a practice of passing the microphone around during the first part of the service and inviting guests to introduce themselves. As the lay service leader announced this time of newcomer intro-ductions, I thought, "Should I say anything? Should I identify us?" Yes, I concluded! This was one of my bottom lines; I needed to be bold enough to test whether there was room for us in this community. The mic came around, and I introduced myself and my partner as a couple visiting for the first time.

Gosh darn it, I'd done it! *Boy,* had I done it. My stomach, already suffering that morning, began to sink further as there was no applause of greeting after our introduction . . . just silence. I sat back down and immediately began imagining the stares and scorn that were probably being directed our way by all the elders seated around us. I barely remember the rest of the worship service. I remember singing some hymns—I quickly read ahead to make sure that the words that were coming up weren't objectionable, which they weren't. I remember there being a sermon, something about community. I remember the whole experience feeling very Christian, even if the content wasn't necessarily so. As the service moved toward its conclusion, I remember clearly thinking, "Well, the content's okay . . . but this was probably a mistake. I'm sure they don't really want us here." I resolved that as soon as the service ended my partner and I would immediately head out the back door. No need to prolong this nerve-wracking experience.

The service ended, I grabbed my partner's hand, and out we headed, down the church's central aisle toward the back doors. Until, that is, one of the grannies in a row behind us shoved her walker into the aisle, blocking my way. She got out . . . looked at me . . . reached out over her walker, and embraced me in a hug, whispering in my ear, "I'm so glad you're here, in our community. Welcome." It was all I could do not to burst into tears right then and there . . . and still, decades later, I weep at remembering how welcome and loved she made me feel in that moment. To me, it was radical hospitality, embodied. Every fear I had about being in that space, with a community I did not yet know, evaporated in that moment of unbridled, unhesitant welcome. Every stereotype I had about elders not accepting gays and lesbians vanished. It was as if my own grandmother were hugging me and welcoming me home after a long absence. It was, in fact, exactly that—a welcome back to spiritual community, after a very long absence.

In the ensuing months, as the congregation began slowly healing from its rift, the rifts in my own heart began to heal as well. I began to rediscover myself as a spiritually oriented human being, and began diving into Unitarian Universalism with a newbie's zeal and enthusiasm. During that first year, as the congregation remained without a senior minister, I was invited several times to be a lay preacher. "Remind us why we're worth finding," one elder said to me. "We need your enthusiasm right now." And so I did. I preached about being Hindu and Unitarian Universalist. I preached about being gay and spiritual. As I did so, a greater wholeness began unfolding within me, one grounded in the things my soul had been longing for, without my even realizing it: spiritual community and a deeper sense of faith. As the tiniest glimmers of a new and different future began taking shape, one of my newfound friends in the congregation commented to me after a Sunday service I led, "We're going to see you in seminary before it's all said and done!" The thought had never occurred to me, but the seed had now been sown—by a fellow UU, in the context of our beloved community.

The power of grace to save us, to move us toward our best and truest selves, even when we don't know what we're looking for or what we need, is amazing and beautiful. What a blessing it is for me that Unitarian Universalism has been a part of the grace that has shaped and transformed my life.

Three Ways Unitarian Universalism Has Helped with My Depression

Kenny Wiley

I'd guessed correctly—our ultimate frisbee tournament opponent's best thrower faked like she was going to throw deep left, then adjusted rapidly, her wrist curling around the disc as she prepared to throw deep and to the right. I was one step behind the man from the other team I'd been assigned to defend. Pouring rain had given way to the blistering June sun. Our ultimate frisbee team needed to stop them from scoring here.

I sprinted one half-step behind my opponent, the two of us chasing the disc as it flew. Fresh mud flew off our cleats as teammates cheered us respectively on. The woman's throw was, as usual, right on target. I'd have to dive. I stuck out my dirt-stained left hand mid-layout, my body fully horizontal. I knocked the disc away just as the man's hands expectantly smacked together. The watching crowd erupted as I landed face-and-chest-first in a puddle of dirt and water.

On contact with the ground, tears immediately sprang from my eyes. I made to get up—the game wasn't over, after all—and then discovered I was just *done*. I had nothing left except my despair. My teammate and long-time close UU friend Bryce helped me off the field, then held me as the tears kept coming. Opponents and team-mates alike thought I'd been badly hurt. I was indeed in tremendous pain—just not from an ultimate dive. What a sight we must have been: two young men, sweating profusely and comically muddy, one weeping uncontrol-lably, the other's left arm slung around the first.

I landed in that muddy puddle three years ago, one of four rock-bottom experiences I've had in my sixteen years with depression. I have since spoken out repeat-edly, on Facebook and in sermons, on the importance of reducing stigma about mental health struggles. I am sometimes asked how my Unitarian Universalist faith helps me combat depression.

I was first diagnosed with clinical depression at age thirteen, after a spiral of anger and lethargy rendered my parents utterly baffled. I would rage—on the tennis court, against my father, and, most spectacularly, against myself. I'd insult myself for hours on end, first under my breath, then in writing. *Why didn't people understand how horrible I was?*

I've come to learn that such vicious self-talk is not my fault. Understanding that depression is largely chemical disequilibrium is intellectually doable; convincing myself deep down takes more work. Perhaps the toughest part of depression—both how it feels within and how it looks on the outside—is figuring out which parts or symptoms "aren't my fault" and for what I must take responsibility.

As my mom observed me throughout my teenage years, she noticed that, while my depression could not be easily "cured," I *could* mitigate the disease's effects through what she and I began to call "The Big 4," after the four rules that governed UU youth rallies in the UUA's Southwest District. When I'd call her, feeling despondent, we'd go over the "Big 4" checklist together:

1. Have you eaten lately?
2. Have you slept?
3. Have you exercised lately?
4. Have you read anything good or learned anything fascinating lately?

Depression robs me of the inclination to take care of myself. *I don't matter, so why eat well or go play basketball?*

When I had a severe depressive episode in the fall of 2006, I focused on doing those four things every day. It didn't fix things immediately, but the ritual of achieving small wins kept the suicidal thoughts at bay.

"You have to decide to feel better" is both obnoxiously trite and entirely true in my experience battling depression. Folks who mean well but don't understand how depression works chalk up defeating it to "you gotta want to." If only! Yet the decision to face it down can, on some level, only come from within. Perhaps the most important thing I have done is to have the courage to let others in—and, through therapy and treatment and experience, figure out how those who love me can be of assistance.

My faith communities and close UU relationships have kept me alive. The story of my ultimate teammate Bryce just sitting next to me as I wept is only one example of how fellow Unitarian Universalists have been willing to simply sit and be with me. A person who refuses to give up on me helps shout down depression's mantra: that I am unworthy and unholy. Those who sit with us in hard times are saying, through their actions, that we are worthy of love.

My depression leads me toward comparison. I compare my current self with the self of three years ago, or a friend, or an unattainable goal. *If I were a good person,*

I would . . . call people back more. Listen better. Be a better partner or friend. Be faster or thinner.

I work as a religious educator in the Denver area; our older elementary children at church have had a series of conversations about depression and mental health. One child wrote, when prompted to ponder how she might console a close one, "You are already good. You are already enough."

You are already good. You are already enough. Through songs and gestures and tear-filled hugs, I have been told that by Unitarian Universalism over and over again. Not always, of course, and we do not say it or live it enough—but at our best, that is who we are. We are the faith of "You are already good. You are already enough."

A few months ago—a couple of years after my dive into the muddy bottom of my despair—I found myself on another rain-soaked ultimate field, playing again with my friend Bryce. This time I was on offense, and he'd thrown the frisbee deep, and in my direction. At first it seemed too far away, but I sprinted hard anyway.

You can get this.

For once, my "self-talk" wasn't negative or falsely positive.

You might not catch this. Run anyway. You might land in a huge puddle. Dive anyway.

I dove—right into a bunch of water—and missed the disc by an inch. People on both teams *oooooh*ed their disappointment. For a moment I let my now-drenched head and face rest on the ground. Lots of water; this time, no tears. I got up and jogged over to Bryce, who shrugged and smiled.

"You okay, man?"

We made eye contact. "I've been worse."

He grinned knowingly, we slapped hands, and kept on playing.

Back from Despair

Ted R. Ogg

The welcoming and nurturing environment that Unitarian Universalism provides has developed in me a sense that I am a spiritual being capable of searching out and sensing the divine.

The world would have led me to a far different conclusion. The conservative, evangelical, born-again theology I'd known as a boy in the Texas Panhandle taught that being gay was an abomination and a straight ticket to hell. God, they said, would not even hear me. Moreover, I could not hope for love in the only way I felt possible. My only slim chance to go to heaven was to live a lie; tell lies about whom or what I loved.

Well, you know what? I didn't really care. I spent my time in the disco. Man, how I loved the late 1980s and early 1990s. The Goth clothes, the bands from Europe, the parties and chemicals never seemed to end. In 1992,

I found out that I was HIV positive. I made up my mind right then to party till I died. In those days there were no really good meds and since I was going to hell, maybe if I partied real hard I'd end up in hell, but I'd still be young and cute. Truth be told, hell sounded so much better than heaven anyway. Sort of like a big old underground club or rave party that never ends. And thus my life went on for years.

In around 2000, a lesbian friend invited me to the Unitarian Universalist Fellowship in Amarillo, Texas. From the very first moment I was intrigued, amazed, and hooked. I took my mom with me a time or two before she passed. I was, for the first time, welcome to more or less be myself. I found a free and responsible search for truth. I found a laid-back, relaxed environment that invited me to light a candle and share my joys and sorrows. I made my deviled eggs for pot-luck Sundays.

Still, I only scratched the surface. I liked partying more than praying. After losing both parents, my life devolved into addiction and chaos. The Texas Department of Criminal Justice became my home away from home. Being incarcerated separated me from chemicals but it left a huge void. It became apparent to me that I wasn't going to a fabulous underground rave anytime soon.

I began going to recovery meetings and worked the Steps. I was invited to develop an abiding faith in a

Higher Power. There is a chapter for the agnostic that encourages us to stop being so hard-headed and see where clergy may offer some real benefit.

I signed up for a faith-based dorm program that lasted a year and demanded classes three nights a week plus a worship service. Except I didn't like or trust mainstream religion. And from somewhere deep within I decided to contact the Unitarian Universalist Fellowship in Amarillo. They, in turn, referred me to the Church of the Larger Fellowship. Immediately I dove into the correspondence courses and got a pen pal from Boston.

The love of this community brought me back from despair. I've learned that not only do LGBTQs belong in church and worship but many have been called to lead. I get very emotional when I read beautiful essays and stories by "my people." Of course now "my people" really includes all UUs, regardless of orientation. And to take that a step further, everyone on this planet, because we truly are a part of an interdependent web of life.

Unitarian Universalism has changed my life in myriad ways. Most of the hurt, anger, and distrust of conservatism has vanished. With a year or so left to serve on my violation I am still dedicated to pursuing the life-changing faith that Unitarian Universalism has helped me develop.

Of course, now as I near fifty, life seems so very good to me that I'd like to hang on to it. Hell no longer seems like a possibility. My belief is that within each of us is a spark, an individuation of the divine. And the Creator would never punish itself. I'm still open to the idea of an eternal rave party surrounded by truth, love, and life. Hopefully for that I can get a good table reservation because I just can't dance like I used to.

Thank you for saving my life, my soul, and for allowing me to share my story.

The Unitarian Universalists Believed in My Inherent Worth and Dignity

Mike Smith

My story is about transformation—change. To appreciate the change that I went through, you need to know what my life was like before 2010.

I was raised a Methodist but it didn't take. In fact, up until I turned thirty-eight I was an all-but-avowed atheist. And it wasn't really easy. Although I had good friends, I felt some separation from them. Then in 1990 I watched Ken Burns's Civil War miniseries and read extensively about the war. I became convinced that some sort of supreme being had to be involved somehow. That made my sense of separation from others even worse. I could no longer identify as an atheist, but my concept of a deity was seriously at odds with those of mainstream religions.

By the mid-1990s I was in my early forties, had been working as a craps dealer in Las Vegas for fifteen years, and had finally become a very respected dealer at a major Strip casino. Although I was still in touch with a few of my high school buddies back in Phoenix, where I had grown up, the vast majority of my friends were co-workers. I had good relationships with many of my fellow dealers. They made it clear that they enjoyed working with me, respected my skill as a craps dealer, and also enjoyed socializing with me outside of work.

At this time I got married to a woman who had been my best friend for twenty years, and who had an eight-year-old son with Asperger's Syndrome. Unfortunately, due to a combination of health issues she died eleven years later. Her son still lives with me, and he is very much my son.

The last years of her life and the first few after she passed were a very difficult time for me, and I started indulging in some risky behavior. A few years later it caught up with me, and I found myself arrested and charged with a felony. I do not wish to spell out the full nature of my felony, but in October of 2010 I spent thirty days in the county detention facility. Prior to this the most trouble I had ever been in was for parking or speeding violations, and now suddenly I was in jail. I was terrified.

After the thirty days, I was released on my own recognizance and given a suspended sentence and five years' probation. I promptly lost my job, and my former co-workers, who had been my friends, would have nothing to do with me. My old high school friends back in Phoenix could do little. My future looked bleak. I was very depressed, with a lot of time on my hands. My house, now with only me and my son in it, seemed very large and empty.

I had extreme difficulty finding work. I was also in therapy, and after about ten months my therapist strongly recommended I find some group—any group—that I could connect with. I had no idea what such a group could be, but I decided to try and find a religious group that I might have at least some common ground with. And because of all of the reading I'd done on American history, the Unitarians came to mind. But I really knew nothing about them and had no idea what I would find. I did a computer search and discovered that a satellite group of Unitarians, connected to the main church in Las Vegas, was meeting very close to my home. So at the end of February 2012 I attended one of the earliest meetings of the Red Rock Unitarian Universalists.

It was a small group of people, only ten or fifteen, meeting in an uncomfortable and uninviting environment —metal folding chairs that were kind of cold (this was

February), tile floors, harsh lighting, lots of distracting background noise—and I can't remember the topic that night. But I do remember a lot of friendly people coming over and talking to me, and I remember joining hands at the end to sing "Spirit of Life." The love and acceptance that I felt at that moment were almost overwhelming. It was only then that I truly appreciated how badly I missed human connection.

Very shortly after that I attended my first UU service at the main church. When I parked in the front lot I noticed a sign on the side of the building: "Different Beliefs, One Congregation." I had found my group.

The people I met were a friendly bunch, and many of them wanted to know more about me. I quickly faced a tough decision—tell the truth or lie. But it really wasn't that tough. I couldn't lie to these people. I reached out to the leaders of the Red Rock group and the main church and had many long conversations with lay leaders and ministers. They agreed that their belief in the first Principle meant they had to accept me. But they also did their due diligence, because the safety of the congregation was their first priority. The ministers have been in continuous contact with my probation officer and my therapist.

For a variety of reasons, everyone agreed to keep my situation confidential. Only people who needed to know were informed. This worked for a while, but then Larry

Jones invited me into his chalice circle—his posse, as we like to call ourselves. At first I kept mum about my situation, but I quickly realized that couldn't continue. How could I not talk about my probation, the most important fact of my life, during the chalice circle check-in? I told my therapy group that I intended to tell my chalice circle everything. My therapy group was horrified. They told me I was crazy. That I'd be rejected, kicked out of the church, let alone the chalice circle. Even my therapist thought it was a bad idea, although she applauded my honesty and forthrightness.

I told them—and received even greater support, acceptance, and friendship than before. I think they should all pat themselves on the back.

Early in 2014 I was charged with a probation violation and reincarcerated. The act in question was something I was responsible for, but didn't do, and when my lawyer, my probation officer, the state attorney, and the judge could all get together, my probation was quickly reinstated and I was released. But that took about three weeks, during which I was in jail again.

But my incarceration this time was completely different. This time I had a solid group of motivated friends on the outside. They visited me, they looked after my son, they wrote to me, and they even pooled money to get me a lawyer. This time I was not terrified. I knew my UU friends would stand by me, and they most certainly did so. And I was greeted with open arms when I got out.

I'm happy to say that I have completely paid back the money that was raised on my behalf, and I am no longer on probation.

I can't say that my UU friends saved my life, but they certainly saved the quality of my life, and that's at least as important. The Unitarian Universalist Congregation of Las Vegas stood by their principles and absolutely walked their talk! They should be proud of themselves, and I'll never be able to adequately thank my UU friends.

Ministry with Integrity

Cynthia A. Snavely

Unitarian Universalism saved my calling. I entered the United Methodist ministry in my mid-twenties, having gone straight from high school to college to theological school. For six years I served a small, rural, two-church parish in the coal region of eastern Pennsylvania. Then I became an assistant minister at a larger church in a resort area, also in eastern Pennsylvania.

Several things happened in the one year I served that congregation that challenged my sense that I was in the right place.

My senior minister often asked why women and African-American clergy had to have their own support groups, and often asserted that clergy who identified as LGBT should be kept out of the United Methodist ministry. I identify as a white, cisgender, straight female, so only one of those comments struck me personally, but all of them contrasted with my sensibilities.

A young male member of the church gave me a set of novels set in "the end times," and spoke of wanting to be ready to fight "on the Lord's side" when those "end times" came. I found such martial, them-versus-us views disconcerting.

Two clergywomen and a layman in the United Methodist Conference published a book about using feminine imagery for Christ, particularly a pre-existent and resurrected Christ. There was quite an uproar, with many of the senior clergy demanding that the two clergywomen be defrocked. I read the book and found the views in it cogent and sensible.

I was working within a system where members of the church did not have a lot of power. Occasionally, a member of the congregation would ask me, "When do we get to vote on this?" The answer within that system was, "You don't."

I worked with three boys on their religious scouting badges, using the United Methodist program. The youngest had a section in his workbook on the Trinity. He said he did not understand the concept and asked me to explain it to him, which I did, but as I did so I realized that I did not think the concept was biblical. I was already a universalist Christian, not believing that a loving God would condemn anyone to hell for eternity.

I was comfortable being a universalist Christian within the United Methodist Church. But now I found myself a unitarian Christian as well.

All of these made me realize that I could no longer serve in the United Methodist ministry with integrity. My superiors within the system told me I could hold the views I did and remain a United Methodist minister, but that did not feel honest to me. And yet I still felt a strong call to ministry. So I wrote to the Unitarian Universalist Association, describing myself as a United Methodist minister with unitarian and universalist Christian views and asked what I would need to do to become a Unitarian Universalist minister.

The first thing I needed to do was to belong to a Unitarian Universalist congregation as a member for a year. So I joined the UU Church of the Lehigh Valley. I was soon invited to take part in the church's pagan women's group, and I was introduced to a Buddhist member of the congregation. By the time the year was up, I was describing myself as a humanist who respected the Christian tradition in which I was raised.

In order to have some income and a place to live, I enrolled in a clinical pastoral education residency in a hospital and served in that capacity for a year. Eventually I was fellowshipped into the Unitarian Universalist ministry. Since then I have served congregations in Pennsylvania, West Virginia, Maryland, and North Carolina, and worked with a UU social justice organization in the Maryland, D.C., and northern Virginia region.

It has felt good to take anti-racism trainings alongside other Unitarian Universalists, to work for the freedom of same-sex couples to marry, to work for human rights for people who identify as transgender, to work for immigration reform and on environmental issues. My Unitarian Universalist colleagues and congregants are always encouraging me to more fully live out my faith by consistently working toward the ideal of beloved community. I have found a ministry that is inclusive and conforms to my understanding of living out the golden rule of loving all my neighbors, not just some.

It feels good to live out my call to ministry with my integrity intact. Unitarian Universalism has made that possible.

My Eureka Moment

Tamara Angelique (AKA Thomas E. Flick)

I was raised in a Christian household and in the United Methodist Church. But the individuals who raised me did not live the faith they claimed. At a very young age, I knew I was different. My attraction for boys and my preference for girls' attire and toys made me a target for abuse from family and friends. I felt ostracized. My Christian upbringing taught me that homosexuality (that's what it was called then) was a sin and that LGBTQ people were bound for hellfire for eternity. Despair and loneliness caused me to rebel against my family as they never would accept me for who I am.

Thus began my search for religion and acceptance, which I had come to learn don't mix in most circles. I delved into countless religions—Catholicism, Lutheranism, Jehovah's Witnesses, Mormonism, Christian Science, Islam, and many more. I even went so far as to conform to the beliefs and practices of each faith. I can't tell you how many nights I spent begging God to remove my desires and feelings from me; if a change like that was necessary for others to love and accept me, then I must change. Needless to say, God never removed any of myself from me. I began to think and believe that no religion or faith group would accept me. I also began to realize that my belief system definitely did not fit into any set creed or doctrinal statement and that I could not belong to any one religion. Then there are my radical political views to consider. As a socialist I am hated and opposed by most religious groups, even though I work toward justice for all, true liberty, and the end of *all* forms of oppression. So, I abandoned all conventional forms of religion and started my own path. My practice consists of many spiritual beliefs, such as those of Buddhism, paganism, theosophy, Edgar Cayce philosophy, spiritualism, and much more. I've found that my spiritual practice is not a set practice, but is ever evolving as my understanding and knowledge grow.

Then, by accident, I found Unitarian Universalism and the Church of the Larger Fellowship. I was in the process of writing to various ministries and groups that offered free pen pals. CLF sent me an information packet about Unitarian Universalism, and I was instantly intrigued. The more I studied, the more I realized that

I've been a UU my whole life and never knew it. That was my eureka moment. Now I belong to a church that accepts me for who I am and nurtures me and assures me of my self-worth. I am encouraged to never compromise who I am and what I stand for on behalf of *any man or thing*! I have learned that my values and strengths matter. I have learned that God cannot fit into any box. God is *too big*! And when it comes to spirituality, everyone has the right to believe how they wish to believe. Our faith is like a patchwork quilt. Each patch is different, but also essential to make up the quilt. This is why I love Unitarian Universalism so much. It embraces the intricate and complex web of existence and all paths of life.

I feel so blessed to have a church home. I feel as though I'm at each service in spirit, taking part in sacred fellowship. I thank each and every one of my fellow UU/CLF members for allowing me to be me and flourish like a fresh rose blooming in the garden of life. I treasure our sacred fellowship, and may we all continue to be one spirit, an intricate part of the divine that is in us and surrounds us. May you all be abundantly blessed.

Namaste, your trans sister,
Tamara Angelique

I Am a Lotus Flower

Devi Pierce

The year 2011 was devastating for me. My life revolved around depression, starvation, paranoia, hospitalizations, therapy, more therapy, and multiple psychiatric medications. I was barely able to focus on my family or my job as a physician. I had had psychiatric issues in the past but had never dealt with anything as intense as this. I was utterly lost and was actively suicidal.

My inner darkness was real, and evil. I had intense hate for myself from an early age. By the time I was sixteen, this hate had driven me to torture myself. I would pound my fists against brick walls until my knuckles were broken. I would pull out my toenails. I would starve myself, and abuse laxatives and diuretics until dehydration meant I could barely walk. My worst crimes against myself, though, were my cuts. I would cut my skin with knives, glass, razors, and scalpels, sometimes to the point of needing twenty or thirty stitches. I belonged to the SI community, the self-injurers, commonly known as the "cutters." Ours is an isolated, barbaric world, but it is nonetheless inhabited by many. This is a secret world as well. We rarely tell you about our pain or illness. We lie about our past and our scars. I have lied about my scars so often that I now believe the lies myself. I have lied on all the applications I have filled out since high school. When they ask, "Do you have mental issues," how should I respond? How can I say that I have inflicted injury on myself over and over? Who would understand or accept that? I have been called crazy, and not as a joke. I learned to keep the extent of my illness secret from most people, including close friends and family. If I had admitted my disease to the outside world I would never have become a physician and would have not been allowed to adopt my daughter. And admitting the extent of my self-hate would only make me ashamed and add to my self-hatred.

In 2011 I desperately needed something to change in my life, but I did not know what to try. I began to think about turning to religion and spirituality. My partner is extremely religious and attends a Presbyterian church regularly, so I thought I could attend there. I went to her church several times, but, though warmly received, I felt nothing but irritation listening to the worship service.

I was raised in an anti-religious household and taught that no organized religion was to be believed in or trusted. But even though my parents hated organized religion, they played bridge with a group of Unitarians. I thought, if my liberal parents can tolerate these Unitarians, maybe I can too. And maybe they even play bridge.

I began searching for information about Unitarian Universalists and their beliefs. I read the seven Principles and, in general, agreed with them. I came to First Unitarian in the fall of 2011, excited but scared. The first sermon I heard was about the Occupy Louisville movement—an odd sermon topic, I thought, but interesting. Everyone told me to come back for other sermons so that I could get the real flavor of the place. I came back. There were more social justice sermons, and on two Sundays we did crafts for social justice issues during the service. At that point, I realized that this was not the church or religion for me.

I was at a crossroads—would I continue to attend, or would I quit? I have never been a quitter, but being at church every Sunday was incredibly difficult for me. Pardon the intensity of this image, but every Sunday I felt like a burn victim whose bandages were being ripped off. I feared exposure and was acutely aware of my illness, shyness, and loneliness. I began to understand more about social justice, but that inner evil continued to eat away at me.

I decided to attend for a few more months, but to get involved in the church—maybe this would make a difference. I greeted at the door and worked as an usher. Slowly, I began to understand the rhythms of a Sunday morning, and these were comforting. I began to develop friendships, and that was a joy. But I had almost given up hope of meeting my spiritual needs.

It has taken me a long time, but I have begun to understand my initial reaction to First Unitarian and to Unitarian Universalism. I had come there to deal with evil. I was looking, truly looking, for salvation, and I was not convinced that I would find it there. There was not much talk about sin, evil, salvation, or grace, and I sensed that these conversations were what I needed.

Then the most amazing thing happened. One day, in a religious education class discussion of gender, I was given a gift: the term *gender queer*. What made it a gift? I was aware at a very early age that I was not a part of "this culture." When I was sixteen I thought I had it figured out. I knew by then that I was a lesbian, and that that made me different from most of my peers. But in that class I realized that I am not cisgender, I am gender queer, and have been all my life. At that moment, I felt I had come home to a real understanding of myself. I am more than just a "tomboy"—I think and act differently because I am not on the gender binary; it has no place for me. Imagine the impact of that revelation. Imagine how that reframed my entire past. Imagine what a truly spiritual, soul-defining moment that was for me.

It was also a moment of grace—an unexpected gift, freely given to me, which had a major impact on my identity and my understanding of my self-hate. I had experienced grace at First Unitarian Church. What? *Grace?* In a religious education class?

In the years I have been at First Unitarian, I have had other moments of grace as well. This essay is based on a sermon I gave to the congregation, and that was a moment of grace. The congregation was extremely supportive. I had officially come out as a person living with mental illness. Imagine that freedom! A freedom I had never been able to experience with any other group of people. I was finally allowed to be myself.

And this grace led to salvation. Salvation can be thought of as deliverance from harm, ruin, or loss. I needed salvation when I came to First Unitarian, although I did not realize it at the time. I needed deliverance from inner evil. In many religions, salvation is obtained by grace that is received from god. Personally, I have not found god at First Unitarian. But I have found free and unmerited gifts and blessings that I never expected. I have found grace over and over. Through this grace I have found salvation. Grace and salvation do not belong only to other religions: they are present in the Unitarian Universalist church as well. Our church, our religion is not just a social justice club—it is much more powerful than that.

Members of the SI community consider the lotus flower our symbol of recovery. The lotus flower grows in ponds, but has its roots in the muck at the bottom. Its stem must grow through this muck before it can blossom at the surface of the pond into a beautiful flower. We in the SI community are frequently stuck in the muck and unable to see the surface. In fact, 10 percent of us will never make it to the surface and will die in the muck. Many others will only grow stems. To surface, to become a lotus flower, is recovery, is freedom.

I am finally growing through the muck and have a few petals on the surface of the pond. I have had many helpers on this journey, but I consider the Unitarian Universalist church to be one of the most important. The UU church has exposed me to grace, salvation, and radical ideas, and in so doing has helped me to escape my inner evil. It has been the milieu of the pond, if you will, which has supported me to grow through the muck.

I now tell people, "Never underestimate the power of this church." I am UU, I am president of my church's board, I am gender queer, I am a person who has suffered and will suffer with mental illness. I am not a self-injurer any more. I am a lotus flower.

With deep gratitude to the congregants of the First Unitarian Church of Louisville and Rev. Dawn Cooley

My Friend, the Unitarian Universalist

Phillip Cory Moore

John and I are in a creative-writing class offered at
our prison by Tulsa Community College. One day as
we discussed the class and our efforts to get our work
published, he explained that a call for submissions
had been issued to Unitarian Universalists to tell how
Unitarian Universalism has changed their lives. He
said that he was going to write such a story and sub-
mit it for publication, to which I said, "I'm not a UU,
but I *know* a UU and *he* has changed my life. Does that
count?"

"Well if it doesn't, it should," he replied.

"I don't know if you could say the changes have
been dramatic, but they certainly have been grammatic,"
I offered, smiling, noting some examples of times he's
helped me with matters of the English language.

For example, he corrects me when I misspeak. He doesn't do it in such a way that it hurts my feelings or makes me feel stupid. It's a learning experience, and I'm thankful that he's willing to take the time to help me improve myself.

John and I were cellmates for a while, and the closeness of living conditions is not unlike some aspects of being married. You end up spending a lot of time with your cellie in very close quarters. Fortunately, John and I got along quite well and, I firmly believe, we learned a lot from each other.

I suspect that some, maybe many, of the traits John exhibits toward me—and others here—are due to his being a Unitarian Universalist. He also follows the teachings of the Buddha and, it seems to me, the combination of the two produces a way of living that is much greater than the sum of the two parts. In particular, he has a knack for maintaining a positive outlook in a very negative environment.

Moreover, he has generally displayed ways of thinking and perceiving the world, and our immediate environment, that I had not considered. It's not that his views are revolutionary. I'd just not been exposed to such ideas about dignity, equality, justice, and spirituality.

In prison, and, from what I've seen, outside of prison as well, many who claim to be religious are not spiritual.

John certainly isn't a religious person, but he is spiritual, and he doesn't just give lip service to it. He lives it. In particular, he sees himself as part of a universal community that takes all beings very seriously, and his community includes way more than just humans.

I do not hide the fact that I don't like spiders, and, before meeting John, I would kill them without a second thought. As my cellie, he asked me not to kill spiders. When one would creep into our cell, John would take over. He has a "capture cup" with a Buddhist mantra, or blessing, written on it. Simply by capturing the spider and putting it close to the mantra, the spider is blessed and will not be reborn in the animal realm, John told me. So he was in charge of capturing and blessing spiders —and I stopped killing them.

Watching him make his spiritual principles part of his life has impressed me. So, I believe that Unitarian Universalism has changed my life.

Coming Home

Kathleen Montgomery

I invented Unitarian Universalism. All by myself. I know numerous other people who have done this as well. I did it on buses, traveling up and down Livernois Avenue in Detroit. I was seventeen or so, a working-class Irish Catholic, living with my parents and attending a Jesuit college about ten miles away. The Jesuits would have been astonished, I suppose, to learn that this was what they had fashioned: a teenager trying to figure out what religion was and could be, and whether it was even possible to be both religious and honest, much less an actual member of an actual church. I thought not. Each day that bus went within a half-mile or so of a Unitarian church, but I didn't know that and, if I had known, it wouldn't have meant a thing.

A decade later in another city, long after I had left "The Church," I stumbled on a passage in a book that described Unitarian Universalism. I was astonished: This thing I had invented actually existed—a richer version than mine, a version with a religious, intellectual, and cultural tradition I couldn't have imagined, but still, identifiably mine. And then there was the experience so many of us have had—of coming home. Of showing up in this church and finding comfort and challenge and people who insisted that I grow, of finding ideas that thrilled and scared me because they demanded so much, of finding a community of scrappy, smart, satisfying people who cared passionately about the church, about Unitarian Universalism, and about leaving the planet a better place, people who believe that they need one another for religious and social reasons, and for the work of making justice.

Unitarian Universalists come from so many places: parents who want their children to be religious but not limited by creeds; community activists who want a religious grounding for their work; people who left a traditional religion because they grew uncomfortable with its message; those with generations of Unitarian or Universalist forebears; gay, lesbian, bisexual, and/or transgendered people who want a church where they will feel welcomed and where their partnerships will be blessed; biracial families; couples from different faiths who join because they want to be married by a clergyperson who will respect and honor their traditions and then decide to stay. Many paths are traveled on the way to Unitarian Universalism.

But what about the folks who don't even know this faith exists, who have some sense of what they wish existed but can't imagine that it does? The kids or young adults or retired men and women on a bus somewhere in some city, longing for something that could be right around the corner or down a street from where they are. What about those people? How does Unitarian Universalism reach them?

Unitarian Universalist churches often exist as small (or sometimes medium-sized or even largish) enclaves of "the chosen." An unspoken feeling seems to exist that if you're smart enough to find us, we'll let you in. Signage is sometimes poor, advertising is nonexistent, and many of us hesitate to invite others to join us at church on Sunday for fear of proselytizing in a way that is disrespectful or pushy. And often we feel unable to find the right words to describe our faith—as though we might fail an exam.

A few years ago I had an experience that changed my feelings about inviting others into my own, chosen, faith tradition. My brother was dying, the sibling I had always been closest to. For months I spent as many weekends as I could traveling from Boston to Detroit. Those weeks were fraught with pain and grief, but also with unexpected moments of something like joy. John and I and the rest of the family cried and laughed together, and odd and amazing things happened, because in the midst of this tragedy, this watching of a marathon runner curled on his bed like a child, there was space only for honesty.

Odd and amazing things happened, but none more odd and amazing than this: Johnny experienced a death-bed conversion. My Roman Catholic brother became a Unitarian Universalist.

He gathered us, his wife, his grown sons, and me, and asked that a friend of mine, Terasa Cooley, then minister of the First Unitarian Universalist Church in Detroit (yes, the very church I had passed decades earlier), be asked to minister to him for his last few weeks and days. The memorial service was held in that church, attended by hundreds of people who couldn't sing the hymns. I smiled, honored to have witnessed this final act of integrity, and pleased to know that he and I were more alike than we had guessed. I was also sad that his life—so rich in most ways—had not been as religiously satisfying as his death. And conscious that the one person who might have changed that was . . . me. I had talked about Unitarian Universalism, of course—it is central to my life—but the one thing I hadn't done, hadn't even thought of doing, was urge him to join me there.

This is what I have learned: For each time I don't reach out to someone who might join this faith, for each time I hesitate to be hospitable, out of shyness or solipsism, I may be leaving someone's life poorer than it might be. If there's a teenager on a bus somewhere—and there is—I'd like to offer her the good news of Unitarian Universalism.

Borderline Child of God

Kelly Murphy Mason

Interesting, what we forget.

At the New England vocational center where staff members, both ordained and lay, assess the suitability of candidates for professional ministry, the psychologist asks me to recall my earliest memory of church. She looks a little like my first therapist, at once kind and weepy. I instantly remember the incident, though I had never thought of it as my earliest experience of church— or even thought of it at all for decades.

> *My childhood home is up the street from Saint Mark's, the only Catholic church on the island. It is brick, boxy, utilitarian, built hastily for I'm not sure whom—summer people? It is the church my family goes to whenever someone is born or dies. That's what I understand of the church, that we emerge*

from it as babies and return to it when we're dead. In the meantime, God lives there; the church is God's house.

On this morning, I walk the three or four blocks to the church by myself. I cannot be more than five years old. Who knows if anyone is looking for me? My tendency, even at this age, is not to say where I'm going when I leave the house; most times, I don't know myself. Today I am going to church alone.

The pews are high and long and fairly empty. I need to sit beside someone big enough to lift and drop the leatherette kneeler, because it is too heavy for me to manage. Midway through the Mass, a stranger's foot kicks up the kneeler, and he and the other strangers file out to receive Communion. I have never received the sacrament before; I know that I have to be older to do that. But I follow the people proceeding single file toward the priest, thinking that surely these are special circumstances.

When the person ahead of me steps aside to genuflect before the altar, I reach my cupped hands out toward the priest. I look expectantly into them, waiting for the Communion wafer to drop there. None does. I look up at the priest. His robes glow white, almost incandescent. He is scowling at me.

"How old are you?" he asks.

In addition to being young, I am quite small for my age; I know that I cannot fake my years. I tell him the truth.

"Go sit down," he says.

I do sit down. Then I slide out of the pew onto the kneeler, and pull myself back up again. I mumble along with the people in my pew. After the mumbling ends, I open the missal to a random page and pretend to sing the hymn that everybody else is singing, but really, I'm just sounding out syllables. When the people start to leave the church, I practically sprint out the doors. Shame gives me speed. Though I don't particularly want to go home, I understand that I cannot stay in that church a moment longer.

The kindly, weepy psychologist cocks her head and asks what possessed me to go to church by myself at that age. I recognize the angle of her face; I realize that she thinks the story is strange. In retrospect, I see that it's a rotten memory, but that's mostly what I have from my early years: rotten memories.

I went a lot of places by myself, I explain. If you're small enough and out in the world, strangers all assume that your mom is the woman with her back turned, or the woman fishing through her pocketbook. Everybody assumes you're somebody else's child. Around my small town in Rhode Island, I got mistaken for somebody else's child quite a bit.

What was that like for me, she wants to know, and I understand that we are going to have precisely the conversation I go to great lengths to avoid.

Did I mention that I'm an orphan?

My family moved to Massachusetts, and my older brother and I were sent to Catholic school because we would get good educations there. The first thing I learned at Catholic school was how to dissemble. My father told us that under no circumstances were we to tell anyone at St. Catherine's that our mother was dead. No one was to know, and especially not the nuns.

If we told people that our mother was dead, the thinking went, they would want to know what happened after she died, and sooner or later, they'd learn that, at ages eleven and ten, my brother and I were already on our second stepmother. Catholic kids were not supposed to have second stepmothers. So we were told to pretend that the four of us had always been a family, mom and dad and kids. Underlying all of this was my father's unyielding insistence that no one should feel sorry for his children. He was almost phobic about our becoming objects of anyone else's pity.

"What do you want, for people to feel sorry for you?" he'd ask with a sneer.

When we enrolled at St. Catherine's, each of us was given a flimsy navy blue book bag with a bright yellow smiley face emblazoned across it. In small letters underneath was the name of the school and its address. I thought that it was spelled out so that if we got lost, people would know where we were supposed to be returned. Between my third- and sixth-grade years, my family moved to three different houses in the Boston area, but St. Catherine's stayed constant, a fixed point on the Massachusetts map. I loved school; so long as I remembered the lies I was supposed to tell, everything would go well for me there.

In religion class, we learned about Catholic doctrine and the Bible, in that order of importance. The Old Testament stories thrilled me. The Israelites stubbornly refused to pretend to believe anything that they didn't actually believe, even if God had asked them to. They didn't have to swallow transubstantiation whole.

One Sunday when we weren't going to church, I told my father that I wanted to convert—that I wanted to be a Jew. Plainly irritated, he told me, "You are not becoming a Jew!"

"Why not?" I asked.

"You tell that to Sister Mary Jane," my father replied

in his most menacing tone. "You tell Sister Mary Jane you want to become a Jew and see what she says. See what kind of grade you get in religion then."

I always got an A in religion. I saw no reason for that to stop. Besides, I didn't know a single Jew who could keep me company.

In the fifth grade, since I was still a Catholic and couldn't become an altar boy, I decided to join the Legio Mariae, the Legion of Mary. My friend Eileen Curley suggested it. Eileen was the seventh or eighth of twelve Curley kids. They all looked like each other; even the parents looked like each other. They obviously belonged together, unlike my family, where the resemblances were faint to nonexistent. The Curleys had all their relatives accounted for; they were all good Catholics.

Kathleen Curley (kid number two or three) was the prettiest girl in the eighth grade, and she had made a vow not only to save herself for marriage, but also never to kiss a boy before she was engaged to him. I knew this because my brother Brian wanted to kiss her. My family truly was the worst collection of Catholics I knew.

But in the Legion, I could pass for a different kind of Catholic, a Curley kind of Catholic. Eileen and I and the other girls would read from the Legio Mariae handbook, then kneel in our polyester plaid jumpers around the card-table altar we had made to Holy Mary, Mother of

God, and pray our plastic rosaries. I said the rosary the same as everybody else, but I was actually praying to my mother, not to Mary.

While I had full faith in heaven, I doubted the existence of hell. I was gradually concluding that it simply did not exist. I confessed my apostasy as I sat beside Eileen on the swing set in her backyard. I did not expect her to be as horrified as she was.

"If we're all God's children, and God loves us so much, then why wouldn't He bring us all home to heaven to live with Him?" I reasoned.

"It doesn't work that way," she said. "All God's children don't know they're God's children, so they don't all go home in the end."

What did Eileen Curley know about children finding their way home? If she ever lost her way, she only needed to follow the nearest kid who looked like her; they'd be like a couple of bees going back to the hive. The Curleys probably did a household headcount at bedtime; with some bitterness, I imagined Mrs. Curley, Queen Bee Madonna, tucking each of her children underneath the covers. I would not be daunted by Eileen's piety this time. "You're wrong. They do so go home," I insisted. "In the end, they all go home."

"That's a sin to say. You could go to hell for not believing in it."

"But I don't believe in hell," I explained, "so I don't care."

Growing desperate, Eileen warned, "You can't be a Catholic if you don't believe in hell."

"Then maybe I'm not a Catholic," I said.

Eileen dug her feet into the dirt, stopped swinging, and glared at me. "Don't ever say that!" she spat. "If you're not Catholic, what are you?"

At that point, I had hardly any idea that Protestants existed, let alone different sorts of them. Only two possibilities existed in my religious universe; if I was not X, than I was Y. Defiant, I told her, "I'm a Jew." I meant it as sincerely as I could.

"Wrong," she said. "Wrong, wrong, wrong. If you're not Catholic, you're nothing."

My maternal grandparents had always hoped that I would someday attend a Catholic women's college, but I disappointed them by matriculating at a prestigious Ivy League school instead. Although the window of my dorm room directly overlooked the luminous steeple soaring high above the campus church, I never set foot in it until my graduation day. In college, after I lost my virginity and started taking birth control pills, I stopped being Catholic and became nothing.

I suppose I thought my sins had reached the tipping point.

My first lover was a nice Jewish boy whose brown eyes reminded me of the cross sections of ancient redwoods. It didn't matter to him that I was a gentile; at Christmastime, he would sing carols along with me. But David was spooked by the medal of the Blessed Mother, a tiny gold disk dangling from a chain that I never took off my neck. In Latin, it hailed the Virgin Mary, Queen of Heaven, who was conceived without sin.

I knew that my dating David bothered a number of our Jewish friends. "So long as you don't marry him, I don't have a problem with it," my Jewish roommate told me. "Now if you get married, that's something different." Of course, at age twenty, I had every intention of marrying him.

Whenever I went home to see my family (which was rarely—I avoided it when I could), my father would ask first, if I was still dating the Jewish guy; second, if I planned on marrying him; and third, if I was going to convert. I replied yes, I couldn't say, and I didn't know. Those replies never fully satisfied him.

In the end, though, I didn't marry David and I didn't convert. Years after our romance had ended, David and I were still close. After I got involved with another Jewish friend of ours who did mind my being gentile, I made an off-handed comment about converting. That infuriated David.

"Don't convert—that's absurd!" he said. "You should absolutely not convert. You're a Christian, Kelly. Okay, so you didn't stay Catholic. Fine. But you're not a Jew, not really. There's absolutely no good reason for you to convert. You love Christmas carols! Why shouldn't you sing them? You like manger scenes with the baby Jesus. I've heard you talk about Jesus; I know what you believe. You should be what you are: a Christian—because that is what you are."

Honestly, I hadn't ever thought of myself in those terms. I had always just been a girl who was constitutionally incapable of playing by the rules of the one holy Catholic and apostolic church; I had little awareness that other churches even existed.

In my seminary bookstore years later, I saw a two-volume work on Saint Teresa of Avila titled *I Want to See God—I Am a Daughter of the Church*. The desire to see God and be seen as God's child was what had drawn me to church at age five. How could the priest who refused me Communion not have guessed that? After a while, I had gotten so used to the church denying me that I stopped asking for God altogether. I figured I probably wasn't the kind of daughter that God would want to see.

The Sunday after my twenty-fourth birthday was a bleak January day that perfectly matched my low mood. My mother had died when she was twenty-three, so my being twenty-four made no sense to me. Despite my deep funk, I decided to go to church. I had not been in quite some time. There was a church a few blocks away from my Washington, D.C., apartment that had its services later on in the morning, a Universalist church on a quiet corner of Sixteenth Street. So that morning, I walked to it. I went alone.

The little I knew about Unitarian and Universalist strands of Christianity, I had learned from books. The little I knew, I liked. Unitarians rejected the Holy Trinity and embraced the oneness of God; Universalists rejected hell and celebrated the oneness of humanity. Unitarians and Universalists saw Jesus as one among countless children of God, announcing the kinship of all in the Kin-dom of God. At this neighborhood church, the Universalists spoke glowingly of "the final harmony of all souls with God."

The minister was a middle-aged man in an academic robe who could just have easily been headmaster at a boys' prep school. He preached a sermon called "The Pillow of Ignorance"; it was a meditation on what we would never know about God. God was not so much an idea as a resting place, the minister explained, an abiding experience of rightness and peace. Whatever we believed about God was almost immaterial; what mattered was that we rested in God. God was larger than our dreams, and sometimes stranger.

The Universalists did not celebrate Communion. Instead, they held a coffee hour after the service. Coffee hour seemed to me a strange Protestant ritual; it held me in its thrall. Coffee and cookies were set out, neatly arranged on trays with doilies. Who knew such tables were still set? Around it mingled good-looking gay men, gray-haired women, and a handful of stray children in their Sunday best. I instantly loved each of them.

Within months, I converted, signed the membership book, and joined the church. I had at last found a place where I could be the kind of Christian I needed to be, in a congregation that had Jews as well as runaway Catholics in the pews.

But I didn't mention any of this to the members of my family, which, as one of my friends joked, had been "Catholic since before the Pope was an altar boy."

My superego stayed Catholic. There was a nagging part of me that associated Sundays with skipped Masses and mortal sin. I went to the Universalist National Memorial Church regularly, and missed a weekend only when I was sick or out of town. The weekend following, without fail, when I shook the minister's hand after service, I made my excuses and apologized profusely.

My family learned of my religious conversion the day my father died. Desperate to inform me, my older brother called my boyfriend's apartment that Sunday morning. My boyfriend told my brother that I was not with him then—that I was at the church. My brother asked, "Which church?" Needless to say, he had never heard of it.

My father died suddenly, but the news did not shock me. In retrospect, I had been waiting for the notification call for years, more and more anxiously as his drinking progressed, but the finality of that call was bracing. My father's funeral was held at the boxy church down the street from my childhood home, the same church where my mother's Mass had been held decades before.

There was no denying that I was an orphan then. I stood up on that chancel where the priest had turned tiny me away from the Eucharist, stood there without any notes, and gave my father's eulogy, which I'm told was beautiful. I hardly remember a word I said. I've no doubt, though, that my father would be proud of me, because from the start of his wake through the funeral Mass and his final interment, I did not shed a single tear, and I never once expected anyone to feel sorry for me.

❦

Just blocks away from the New York City seminary I attended, a man on the corner routinely begged for money. For a few reasons, I never quite believed he was homeless: he usually dressed for the weather; he had a variety of outfits; and his clothes were always fairly clean. Perhaps this was my needed fiction: that he had a place to go to late at night, a home where someone did his laundry and noticed what he wore. I guess I needed to believe that he wasn't altogether alone. Some days the man was aggressive; other days, merely plaintive. Most days, he seemed out of his mind.

One day, when I passed him, he shouted to me, "I might be a borderline child of God."

That tagline stopped me in my tracks. "Me, too," I said.

"That's a rarity," he observed. "Strange things happen."

Ever afterward, I felt a real bond with this man. I usually gave him a little money or offered to buy him something. He was savvy; he always staked out the corner in front of the street vendor's stand. On one day in late summer, he stood there wailing, "Won't someone please buy me a drink? It's so hot, and I'm so thirsty."

Pausing by the vendor's, I asked the man what he

wanted. I took an orange soda out of the cooler and handed it to him. As I reached to take my change from the vendor, I heard him behind me wailing again, "Won't someone please buy me a drink? It's so hot, and I'm so thirsty."

He hadn't opened the orange soda. I tried explaining to him that he was holding an ice-cold drink in his hands. He glanced down at it, suddenly surprised.

Halfway down the block, I heard him once again wailing, "Won't someone please buy me a drink? It's so hot, and I'm so thirsty." Looking over my shoulder, I saw him waving his orange soda through the air, his other hand outstretched for change. Maybe this is a tendency all we borderline children of God have: to stay thirsty or hungry even when we don't have to anymore.

Strange things happen. We forget we've been fed, or we refuse to drink. We all develop certain habits, I suppose. I spend so much time in churches because I'm trying to break a few of my worst. I go to church hoping to see those bad emotional habits break like bread over wine. Today the adult me goes seeking Communion as surely as the child.

Not too long after my ordination to the Unitarian Universalist ministry, I married my Jewish fiancé in the seminary chapel of my alma mater, in an interfaith service with a rabbi and minister co-officiating under the chuppah our friends had loaned us for the wedding. Neither Ben nor I was converting. My two brothers walked me down the aisle, and my maternal aunt lit a candle in memory of my deceased mother and father. What still stays with me from that lovely ceremony is my sense that nothing—nothing whatsoever—was missing from it. I had almost never felt that before.

None of us wants to wander the world alone. Even now, the habit I hate most in myself is the habit of cosmic loneliness. It dies hard for me. It dies—when it does, if it does—somewhere in the shelter of God's house, and the one thing I've tried very hard to remember is my way there.

Carl Scovel Saved My Life

Roger Butts

Carl Scovel saved my life. Well, more accurately, a single paragraph of forty-five words written by Carl Scovel in a four-hundred-page book, *A Unitarian Universalist Christian Reader*, saved my life.

I'll explain. In 2002, I was called to be the minister at the Unitarian Church, Davenport, Iowa. In Davenport, my wife and I had three children. I had good friends. I knew successes. We started Progressive Action for the Common Good, a community organizing group. I worked closely with the local interfaith clergy group on many issues, local and national. We went from symbolic acts of support for the LGBT community to legally binding same-sex weddings.

While in Davenport, I also experienced difficulties around the art and science of being a senior minister. I was scattered. I engaged in struggles with people I imagined weren't on board. I was sensitive to criticism. I grew depressed. Things only got tougher at my second church, in Colorado Springs. My shortcomings collided with a congregation that was not a good fit for me, as I was not for them.

After eleven years, my time as a senior minister was over.

After leaving parish ministry, I entered into dark, difficult times. The dark night of the soul is nothing new, but when it is yours, it sure feels exhausting. I wavered between cynicism and despair. And all those books about learning to walk in the dark are right: You learn things in the dark that you'd never discover otherwise.

My wife, my friends, and fellow clergy (UU and otherwise) were helpful. And one thing that enabled me to move forward was my faith, my strange, hybrid, Unitarian Universalist Christianity. My faith faltered occasionally. It took some hits. It bent in strong winds. It disappeared occasionally. It adjusted, adapted, found new avenues, made new inroads. That whole post-resignation time period was one big heartache, and it required all the resilience I could muster.

In such times, you learn about what abides. The thing I returned to over and over was a single paragraph I had preached on many times over the years. A single paragraph from Carl Scovel's 1994 Berry Street essay,

"Beyond Spirituality." I discovered it in a huge volume put out by the Unitarian Universalist Christian Fellowship. That essay was one of more than three dozen in the book. That paragraph was like a needle in a haystack, but I swear it was as if it were written in neon and flashing off the pages.

That paragraph saved me in that time. I found it comforting. I found it challenging. I found it life-affirming. And it was the constant in the storm. It was lighthouse and life jacket. It showed me the path home. This paragraph:

> The Great Surmise says simply this: At the heart of all creation lies a good intent, a purposeful goodness, from which we come, by which we live our fullest, to which we shall at last return. And this is the supreme reality of our lives.

If it was true of all creation that there was a good intent, a purposeful goodness, through which we could live our fullest, most authentic lives, it was true of me too. I was part of the goodness. I was part of that supreme reality, even if my identity as a senior minister of a tradition I loved was no longer true. Something else was true, even so: I could be that goodness. I could live out of that goodness. And I could reimagine my life, with that image seared into my soul.

Sometime in the 1990s, somewhere in Washington, D.C., when I was alternating between All Souls Church and Universalist National Memorial Church, I discovered this essay and along with it the UU Christian Fellowship. When I needed one thing—any thing—to help me survive the tidal wave of my lost identity, this paragraph came back to me, still fresh and still powerful and still life-giving, two decades later. I think Carl Scovel kind of saved my life, saved my ministry, allowed my faith to endure and to deepen, even in the hardest times.

I am now a full-time staff chaplain at a hospital in Colorado Springs. And what guides me every day as I confront tragedy, tears, resilience, and hope is the idea that every person I encounter holds a goodness, a purposeful goodness, at the very core of their being too.

Emptying My Shoe

Suzi Chase

How did I get here?

How could I have gone so quickly from a warm loving family to a barren empty flat?

Those questions echoed in my mind's dank chambers as I surveyed the unfamiliar living space. Floor-to-ceiling stacks of boxes obscured stark, bare walls. Could the pieces of my shattered life ever reassemble into something resembling normal? Nothing was normal, and maybe never would be again after the metaphorical hurricane that had laid waste to my life.

That hurricane had a name. Transgender.

The media would have you believe transgender people "always knew" their gender. The news shows us story after story of little girls knowing in their hearts they are boys, or boys asking to wear dresses and play with Barbie dolls. Even if this knowledge goes unexpressed for decades, we're led to believe, their gender was obvious to them from a young age.

People are far more comfortable allowing the messy business of a gender transition if it is presented by storytellers as a foregone conclusion from the start.

But reality is nowhere near that neat. I spent the first fifty years of my life with no earthly clue I might be transgender. I had a typical boyhood, laying out plastic soldiers on my floor in imaginary battle scenes and brandishing the toy Western-style pistol I was given for my sixth birthday. An observer might have found my teenage preference for female friends unusual, but I did not. I knew most boys became attracted to girls as teens, and I was no exception. I figured my preference was an effect of that attraction. Throughout my high school and college years, it caused me no problems. Teenage gender norms and those of the liberated era in which I was raised allowed anyone to be friends with anyone else, and I put together a rich social life.

Things changed after graduation. People began pairing off, and social overtures toward single women were generally interpreted as romantic. Finding friendship among females became more challenging. However, I made the best of my opportunities, getting married and raising two children. I was mildly uncomfortable with my role as husband and father, but since I had never really felt like I fit in anywhere, that seemed unsurprising and certainly not an indication of anything unusual about my relationship with gender.

As a married man, I found that developing friendships with women was nearly impossible. I couldn't come up with any way of approaching women socially without looking like I was interested in an affair. Luckily, my wife and I were great friends, keeping the loneliness of my married years partially at bay. I had family and career to keep me busy, so it was not until age fifty that I turned my focus toward the gaping holes in my social life.

I set about putting together the puzzle pieces of what until then had seemed unrelated traits. My reading habits involved almost exclusively books written by, for, and about women. While awaiting the doctor, I invariably chose the women's magazines. My favorite movies featured stories about strong women who overcame adversity, and my favorite songs tended to be those from female artists whose mighty voices sang of feminine empowerment.

I also began for the first time to examine a feeling I'd had since my teen years: regret that I was not born female, with a female body. This yearning never caused me undue distress. I was not ashamed of it, accepting it the way we all accept inevitable reality. Other guys come to realize they'll never be rock stars or astronauts.

I accepted I would never be a woman. That is not to say the desire wasn't powerful. I would frequently try a thought experiment: Would I give up everything to magically become a woman? It was a safe question, given that I knew such transformation was quite impossible, but the answer invariably came back "yes." I would gladly trade my own life for just about any female one.

My wife supported my explorations until the clues began to suggest I might be transgender. "If you transitioned, I'd probably leave you," she told me one night, and I did not object. I certainly would have been upset to find myself suddenly married to a man, and I understood why remaining in a marriage with a woman would not be her choice.

So I was cautious. I tested the waters, first presenting as a woman in public and then joining a transgender-friendly women's reading group. A realization took shape: I was far more comfortable as my female self. Female social interactions seemed "right" in a way that male interactions never had. I began to see my female life as the "real me," while the prospect of spending the rest of my days as a male looked unbearably dreary. I have since learned that current science seems to indicate gender is wired into our brains before we are born. Generations of psychiatrists, psychologists, doctors, and counselors of all stripes have tried and utterly failed to find therapies that consistently allow transgender people to be comfortable with the gender they were assigned at birth. My own experience was consistent with those findings. I was conscious of a part of my being that demanded I be true to it by living as a female. I could no more change it through an effort of will than I could my height or eye color.

However, many whom I took into my confidence urged me to save my marriage by remaining in my male life and avoiding disrupting my family. I had survived a half-century as a male, surely I could survive the rest of the way.

After much soul searching, I still couldn't agree. Imagine you are on a long hike, feet throbbing with discomfort. You soldier on, because everyone on the hike is complaining. But then you all take a break, and you find that your shoe is full of pebbles, while everyone else's shoes are clear. You realize that, though no one's feet feel fine, it's been far worse for you than for others. A simple solution exists—remove your shoe and empty out the pebbles.

What would you say to those who remind you that you've hiked this far, surely you could hike just a little farther? That the hike is more than half done, and you'd inconvenience everyone else, who would have to wait for you to untie your shoe and then lace it back up again? What would you do? Would you just finish the hike, knowing that every step will hurt, or would you beg their indulgence while you emptied your shoe?

In the end, I reluctantly and with much trepidation decided that, while I wished I could have remained as I was for the sake of my marriage, it was asking too much of me to insist that I spend the rest of my life pretending I was someone I'm not. I needed to change, and if my wife left me because of it, I couldn't control that and shouldn't try.

That decision shattered our marriage. After months of vitriolic wrangling we decided she would buy my half of the house. My daughter, then a junior in high school, remained living with her. I moved into my own place, my wife furious that I'd chosen transition over her. My son was away at college by then, so for the first time since getting married I was living alone.

I had been cast from paradise. My new fabulous life as my female self had come down to barren walls and brown cardboard boxes. I posted on Facebook, asking whether anyone wanted to keep me company while I unpacked. The lack of takers came as no surprise—I'm savvy enough to know the difference between Facebook friends and true friends. Though the former numbered in the hundreds, the latter was an achingly small group. My next post, "I miss my family," garnered a cascade of comments but no phone calls.

I needed to rebuild my life. But where to begin? How could I find a place where my brand of newly minted femininity would be supported?

Some weeks earlier, I had attended a gathering of transgender people at the First Unitarian Universalist Church in Baltimore. There, I had run into someone I had worked with years earlier. She wasn't transgender, but was there as a member of the church. She was eager to give me a tour of the historic building, including the magnificent sanctuary where Channing gave his famous sermon. When she learned that I didn't know the first thing about Unitarian Universalism, she gave me a brief primer and read me the seven Principles. I recall thinking it was remarkable that they seemed to express almost precisely my own personal values.

However, I was raised Jewish, a religion that sees itself as under siege since its inception. Jews are trained to resist the draw of other religions, seeing conversion as a betrayal of not just our faith but our very culture, our families, friends, and traditions. So I had filed my knowledge of the UU Principles among the general factual trivia that clutters my mind.

During those early days of living alone, though, feeling adrift and disconnected, the idea of joining a faith community began to seem attractive. I looked into some of the Reform Jewish congregations in the area, but I was not enticed. They appeared more focused on the observance of rituals than any real spiritual exploration.

I got a much different impression visiting the website of our local UU congregation, the Unitarian Universalist Congregation of Columbia, or "UUCC" to pretty much everyone. I found myself registering for a Get Connected class, and on a windy February morning I took a seat in a makeshift circle of chairs at the center of a seemingly cavernous sanctuary in Columbia's Owen Brown Interfaith Center. By the time the class started there were ten women seated there, and we were joined by a young couple a few minutes later. The first order of business involved introductions. As we went around the circle, I was astounded to find that among the ten original women, five of us were queer, including the assistant minister leading the class.

What I heard that day convinced me that UUCC was a great fit. I left intending to take advantage of all the social, spiritual, and educational opportunities I had time for. The only events I planned to skip were the weekly religious services. My childhood memories of synagogue involved excruciating hours listening to interminable chanting in Hebrew about the greatness of God. The only spiritual experience they seemed to offer me came from the overwhelming relief when they were finally over.

While leaving the Get Connected class, I said as much to one of my fellow students, who also came from a Jewish background. She persuaded me to give the service at least one try. So on a Sunday morning in early March of 2014 I first heard the senior minister, Paige Getty, preach.

The topic that week was "family," and the service included testimony by members of three dissimilar families. One involved a blended family and the trials and rewards of merging their two households. A single woman told of her life, and a gay man spoke of initially being rejected but then finally accepted by his partner's mother. Reverend Paige painted an expansive view of the world, one where diverse family structures contribute to beauty and variety. So sincere and affirming was her message that my eyes weren't dry for a moment during the entire hour-long service.

Fast-forward to the present, and nearly every friend I have I met at UUCC. I never miss a chance to hear Reverend Paige preach if I can help it, and I look forward all week to the lazy lunches after services, discussing the sermon, current events, and what's going on in our lives, or just kicking back and enjoying our food. When I had gender-confirming surgery later that spring, I came out as transgender to the entire congregation during the sharing of joys and sorrows. I spoke of my excitement and fear, and I was met by an outpouring of support and a promise from a lay member of the Pastoral Care Committee to call me frequently during my recovery period.

As I write this, I have just returned from three days at a spiritual center after participating in the annual UUCC women's retreat. During one of the fascinating workshops there, it occurred to me how amazing it was to bask in the love and support that warmed that all-female space. And how unremarkable it felt that no one had ever questioned whether, as a transgender woman, I belonged there. The subject simply hadn't come up.

I can't imagine where I'd be had I not found UUCC. My life would certainly lack much of its richness. I teach religious education classes at our Sunday school every week, have helped lead services, and have participated in reflection groups, fun feasts, game nights, and other events too numerous to name. The dark, lonely period after my separation now seems a distant memory. However, I haven't yet found a new romantic partner. Most members of the dating pool in my age bracket appear to accept me as a woman in all ways except eligibility for romance. To them, it seems, I am almost completely female, but not quite enough to date. Fortunately, throughout my dating frustrations and misadventures, my friends at UUCC continue to be a source of constant support.

I Am Not Alone

Devalois LeBrón

It all began when I was reading a book on humanism—
my journey of the desperate search to relieve my soul
and revive my inner spirit. One thing led to another
and I found the Church of the Larger Fellowship.
What I came to discover was that the CLF was what I'd
been searching for all my life. Growing up in a family
of Roman Catholics was more a curse than a blessing
for me. When I was four years old, I knew there was
something different about me. I was born bisexual, and
at age four cute boys and girls caught my attention.
For some crazy reason I thought, why do I want to kiss
them both? Then, while attending school, I realized
that my sexuality was not accepted by my peers, and
that created an invisible wall between the world
I wanted to live in and the world in which I was living.
Eventually, like many LGBTQs, I turned to alcohol

and drugs to escape the world that so much resisted my kind.

I don't want to make this a long letter about myself because this isn't just about me, it's about us all. When I discovered the CLF and wrote to the prison ministry, I took a chance to see what would happen and opened up to a Unitarian Universalist member, Mandy Goheen. When she answered my letter and told me that I was accepted and welcome to become a member, I could not stop crying, because I had finally found not only friends, but a new family that loves, cares, understands, and accepts me for who I am, and who I was born to be. If there is a God out there, he lives in the souls of UU members, we are his most precious children that he has ever created, and God's love is expressed by every member of the CLF. Today I don't see myself as a Roman Catholic, I see myself as a child of the Most High God who has finally found his true home. Thank you! I cannot express, without shedding tears of joy, how grateful I am to have found you. . . . And yes, let the world know that I, Devalois LeBrón, am a bisexual man and am proud to be one, more proud today than ever. Why? Because I know that I am not alone, I have a beautiful family and am a member of the CLF, my home. I love you all, and wish you all great blessings, and if there's anyone out there like me I invite you to come home. We at the CLF are waiting for you, you are family also and we love you, too!

Better Later Than Never

Sharon Peddy Baker

I was past seventy when I discovered Unitarian Univer-salism. I had been searching for a place to worship for several years. I was raised a Methodist, and my friends were all other white Protestant children. I don't think we even had a Catholic church in our town, and I had never heard of a synagogue.

When I was a young mother in a strange town, feeling emotionally abused and longing for my life as it had been, a Baptist minister came to my door. He prayed with me and offered me "salvation." I thought I got it. But I was worried because my parents both smoked and drank alcohol, so I was sure they were doomed. But I never bought the ban on dancing!

It was several years later when I started attending a non-denominational church, and for several years I read the Bible. Actually I read the entire Bible in a year. I kept copious notes during sermons and prayed every day. I was concerned when my daddy died, and I wasn't sure if he was going to heaven. Then the minister of that church left and I lost my faith.

When I moved to a larger town later, I joined a Methodist church because I liked the sermons. Then that minister left and once again I didn't know where to go or what to do. So I didn't do anything.

Several years later I went to a memorial service for a dear friend, and the minister who spoke was the local Unitarian Universalist minister. I couldn't wait to get to that fellowship and hear him again . . . and again and again. But it wasn't just him. I know that now, because he left last year, and I still want to be there every Sunday. It is where I have belonged all along.

I don't feel "guilty" anymore because I enjoy a few glasses of wine and I've been divorced and I've "sinned." I don't feel the need to be forgiven. I don't believe in heaven or hell. I think the Bible is just a book of stories. I am at peace with the feeling I have when I am surrounded by others who do not judge, and who believe *love* is the most important thing we can do.

I just wish I had gotten here when I was seven.

The Ultimate Fighting Church

David McBreen

My life as I knew it stopped in May of 2002. I was arrested and lost the best friends I ever had, my children. I had already lost their mother prior to this, my other best friend. I was suffering from everything from OCD and major depression to PTSD and then some. At that time I had a cellie who introduced me to the Unitarian Universalist faith. I grew up Roman Catholic! I then realized how many religions there are. I opened my mind thanks to the Church of the Larger Fellowship. I now believe that when the gates of paradise are open to us, they will have bleachers on each side with all the different faiths cheering on those that have made it. To me UUs are fighting for all faiths. I call them the UFC—the Ultimate Fighting Church! We are all trying to get to the same place, some of us just take different paths to get there. It's where we are in the end that counts. Love you *all*.

Unitarian Universalism Helped Me Find My Awesome

Melanie Christiansen

Labeling the school-aged me an introvert would have been an understatement. I was the girl who didn't talk in class, or at least didn't talk to the teachers. My mom called me bashful. On the rare occasion when I did force myself to converse with an authority figure, my face would flush, my skin would crawl, my stomach would cramp, and my heart would race as tears uncontrollably spilled out of my gray-blue eyes and down my freckled cheeks.

Fast forward to middle age, when my daughter was about seven years old. She was very curious, eager to try out this "church" thing that her friends were talking about. I was thirty-nine and hadn't attended church regularly since I was six.

About that time, I heard an advertisement on the local NPR station talking about First Unitarian moving to a street not four blocks from where we lived. I had some familiarity with the liberal concepts they espoused, and the timing was impeccable. They were welcoming a new female minister, and lots of exciting things were happening.

My daughter clung to my side during that first service. I attempted to go unnoticed and hoped she would be bored enough to lose interest in church.

We were greeted heartily.

One of my many worries was the singing, since I can't carry a tune. The opening hymn that day is still my favorite: "Love Will Guide Us," by Sally Rogers. "If you cannot speak before thousands," it assured me, "you can give from deep within you. You can change the world with your love." I don't remember if I realized it right away, but I was definitely home.

My next step was to volunteer in the office while kiddo was at school. They needed help, and I had time on my hands. It was nice to be with adults. This allowed me to begin meeting people and feel more comfortable in the building. Slowly, I realized that I would not burst into flames simply from talking to one of the ministers! I attended a membership workshop and met admirable people who went out of their way to connect with me and my daughter. Eventually, I stood in front of the full sanctuary to have my child dedicated on Christmas Eve. To my great surprise I neither peed my pants nor fainted!

While I avoided the vicinity of the pulpit at all costs, I started to feel like part of the community, not just a helpful visitor or an imposter lurking in the back row. Eventually, one of my new friends, David, suggested a terrifying prospect—that I take my daughter to Summer Institute (SI), a weeklong educational retreat on a college campus a few hours from home with about five hundred strangers. By this time, on the advice of another church, I had started to see a personal therapist. Not realizing yet how these things worked, I admitted to him that I had been invited to this event that was so outside of my comfort zone, I hadn't even known it existed until now. Of course, he encouraged me to go. And that's where I found my "Awesome."

I had been to Disney World a year or two before, but there is no magic like SI magic. Here we were, in a tiny college town in Ohio, stacked into dorm rooms for the first time (I had been a commuter student in college). As we checked in, my anxiety was in overdrive. A kind man distributing nametags asked me, "What brings you from Toledo to Summer Institute?" and I blurted out that my friend David had twisted my arm. My greeter laughed heartily. I later discovered he was my minister's dad and was familiar with David's enthusiasm. Connection!

And we kept meeting people. Kind, open people who were not holding back. Radically hospitable people with open arms, loving us just the way we are, not hiding anything, and not wanting us to be any more than who we are at our very core. People with crazily-colored hair, tattoos, shaved, unshaved, comfortable people being themselves. It was impossible not to make connection after connection.

We did church every morning and every evening. So much church. All day long there was spiritual practice everywhere: yoga, meditation, art, board games, and laughter. We found meaning and community in everything. In the late morning of the first day, kids bravely went to classrooms away from parents, confident that they would be treated with the utmost loving kindness. Adults then filed into our theme talk, "Rebooting Your Theology." I hadn't even realized yet that I had a theology! But the connections . . . that's where they were first uncovered.

Somewhere along the week, the combination of unity, individuality, learning, worship, education, radical hospitality, friendship, soul-searching, fellowship, food, and more led me to realize that the first Principle of Unitarian Universalism applied not only to "everyone," but also to me: "We affirm and promote the inherent worth and dignity of every person." That's not just about how I treat others, it's about how I treat myself. It's about how others treat me. I have inherent worth and dignity. I had listened to a hundred sermons by then, but I finally felt it that week at my first Summer Institute. All the listening from all my life came to a sudden comprehension: *I am worthy*. I made a conscious decision then to closely monitor and rewrite my self-talk. What advice would I give a friend or family member in the same situation? Apply to self liberally, repeat as necessary.

Now few people think of me as shy or quiet. Over the last several years, I have led committees and events and participated in Sunday service. I have been on our congregation's board of trustees and made my voice heard. My anxiety is a part of my physiology that I will always need to work through to meet my goals, but I have come to realize that I'm worthy of the effort.

At a subsequent SI, I wrote my statement of faith and read it confidently in front of friends and strangers. I didn't cry, I didn't shake—it didn't kill me. I didn't even have a podium to hide behind. That document continues to evolve, as do I.

Had I not found Unitarian Universalism, I don't know that I would ever have come to the realization that our flaws are sometimes the flip side of our superpowers. I call it my "Awesome" because as I began to emerge from my shell of anxiety, I picked up the catchphrase

"That's awesome!" whenever I found another concept that engaged my new-found enthusiasm. The change in my relationships has been noticeable. It did not take much prodding to convince my niece and nephew to start calling me "Auntie Awesome," which came in handy when I was tasked with creating my superhero name at yet another Summer Institute.

In 2016, I confidently attended my first UUA General Assembly.

Before Unitarian Universalism, I sat in the back of life's classroom, hoping not to be called on or recognized, for nearly forty years. Today I am stationed at the front of the welcome table, understanding the first-timer's anxiety and helping them to find their own natural connections to the church, and helping my church to find those valuable connections to the larger association. People who "knew me when" find it hard to believe that I am feeding the hungry, helping homeless people find services, marching and singing to counter-protest Westboro Baptists, and considering taking steps to become a commissioned lay leader. Without Unitarian Universalism, the term "leader" wouldn't apply to me.

A Perfect Match

Bruce Robinson

I was born in Toronto, Ontario, in 1936. My family attended a local congregation of the United Church of Canada. I recall three noteworthy religious events from my childhood. The first was in Sunday school, when the Bible story for the week was Noah and the great flood. All the students were given the same assignment: to draw a picture showing their impression of what the flood was like. The other students in the class all produced pictures of an ark; most had the standard pair of giraffes poking their heads and necks above the deck. I drew a picture of an innocent child drowning, with an ark in the distance that was out of reach.

The second occurred in a later class when the students were asked to draw a picture of the ancient Hebrews' exodus from Egypt. Again, the drawings fell into two types: everyone else drew Moses with his arms outstretched, and a pathway through the waters opened up in front of him, providing an escape route for his people. In contrast, my picture showed an Egyptian slave couple holding their dead first-born child, whom the angel sent by God had just murdered.

Looking back on these two Sunday school events now, with the perspective of almost seven decades of living, it became obvious to me that I just was not cut out to fit comfortably into even a liberal mainline Christian denomination.

The third event occurred one Sunday morning when I was in my mid-teens, and my entire family was attending church. It was Communion Sunday. The minister deviated from standard church policy and invited not only members of the church, but also those who were planning on joining the church in the near future, to engage in the ritual. When the trays of grape juice and bread came down my row, I made a snap decision. Having no desire to join the church, I passed up the elements of Communion. The mood at home was decidedly frosty for a few days.

Even though I had no interest in becoming a United Church member, I was fascinated by religion itself. I privately studied the major religions of the world. This led me to realize that I had never really sensed the presence of God in my life, or his involvement in the rest of the world. I also studied all the classical proofs of God's existence, and none seemed convincing.

By coincidence, the magazine *Liberty*, which was delivered to my home weekly at that time, began a series of articles written by people with a wide variety of religious beliefs. The first week brought an article titled "Why I Am an Atheist." The author expressed strong convictions that no deities could possibly exist. I was unconvinced.

The next week, the lead article was "Why I Am an Agnostic." This seemed to be a much better match to my beliefs. And the article the third week was "Why I Am a Unitarian." I read that article through a number of times. It was a perfect match! It taught a novel concept: that the purpose of a minister is not to tell people what to believe and how to act, but to help the members of the church derive their own systems of beliefs and ethics.

The next Sunday, I attended service at the First Unitarian Congregation of Toronto. By then I had read more material on the faith, and was moved to join the congregation at the end of the service by signing the membership book.

That congregation was my church home for only a year or two. In 1959, I graduated from the University of Toronto and moved to Kingston, at the other end of Lake Ontario. There I became active in the Kingston Unitarian

Fellowship, which met weekly in a room at Queen's University. I headed its Social Action Committee for some years.

I spent almost forty years as a POM—a plain, ordinary member of the congregation—until my retirement loomed. My father had always stressed the importance of retiring into some new pursuit that was intellectually challenging. He had been a senior executive in a Canadian chartered bank and had seen too many of his fellow executives retire from a high-pressure bank position, put their feet up, watch TV, drink beer, and die quickly.

At the time, the country of Yugoslavia was breaking apart in civil war. Followers of Roman Catholicism, the Orthodox Church, and Islam were battling with each other for control. TV newscasters described the fighting as an "ethnic conflict." I felt very strongly that it was more a religious conflict driven by mutual intolerance. What this world needs, I thought, is more religious tolerance.

The Internet was in its infancy at the time. At the end of 1994, there was no Amazon, Google, PayPal, or Wikipedia. In fact, there were fewer than three thousand websites, and only about 45 million Internet users. My background was in electronics and computers, and it occurred to me that I could create a website devoted to promoting religious tolerance. I founded the Ontario

Center for Religious Tolerance, intending its website to offer perhaps seventy essays, each dealing with a major world religion. The site went online on April 9, 1995.

The website is still live today, at www.religious tolerance.org. A few unsolicited emails arrive daily from visitors. The ratio of positive to negative comments has remained more or less constant over the years, at about three to one. A few of the negative ones have contained death threats that would curl your hair! But many of the positive ones have been very encouraging.

By the end of 2016, three decades after its founding, the originally envisioned seventy essays had grown to about seven thousand, and the site received about a million visitors per month. I remain a Unitarian and an agnostic to the present time.

A Spiritual Journey

Kathy White

What brought me to the Unitarian Universalist Church West (UUCW)? I spent years striving to find a church that would accept me. When I came out as a lesbian, my spirituality became confused and full of questions. Did I still believe in God? Could I be Christian and gay? Would I just be tolerated in church, rather than truly welcomed? Would I go to hell when I died? Was I a sinner because I loved women? Where were God and Jesus on all these questions? Could I love Jesus and be gay?

I faced rejection, ridicule, loss of friends, and minimal tolerance in my religion of origin. I began to question what kind of God would create me this way, then condemn me to hell for living out my love for women. My Christian friend called me an abomination. A minister told me to leave my lifelong religion. I began to drift from church to church, wanting a spiritual home, yet finding emptiness and exclusion wherever I turned. I loved Christian ritual and didn't want to let it go. At times I wandered aimlessly, wondering how God could love heterosexual people so much and despise me. I grieved as I decided to stop going to these places of worship I had loved for so long, and I began letting go of religion, belief in God, and faith in the divine.

But no matter how hard I tried to stop needing a spiritual community, I still kept looking for somewhere to belong. Then I tried UUCW in December 2005. The service was very different from my past religious experiences. I had never seen a woman minister. It felt so freeing to be with people who genuinely welcomed me, honored what I believed, and accepted my sexual orientation easily. The warmth of the minister and the congregation felt very healing, and I began showing up weekly. It wasn't long before my significant other started coming with me. We both basked in the friendliness and acceptance of Unitarian Universalists. I marveled at how I could hold my partner's hand during the service. It was so heartwarming to announce our anniversary during Joys and Concerns and be applauded. Not only was I healing spiritually, but I was also recovering my dignity and self-worth.

I was struck by the joy I saw in the children. They looked happy to go to their religious education classes and clearly enjoyed a freedom of thought I had not seen in my old experiences of church. And the music uplifted and thrilled me. What inspiration I felt listening to lyrics about justice, freedom, compassion, and social action! Gradually I started singing along, meeting more Unitarian Universalists, and joining some groups. When Unitarian Universalist orientation classes were offered, I went and learned about our church's story, our martyrs, and our long history of social justice work. I began feeling proud of this small group of courageous heretics who lived authentically and justly. In February 2006, I gladly signed the membership book and officially joined the congregation.

Being a UU felt like coming home. I had always been a seeker and a questioner. Now I found myself among a diverse group of pagans, Buddhists, Jews, Christians, atheists, and humanists. We were a community of seekers who lived in the questions and formulated meaning without a creed. I was free to express my opinions, listen respectfully to others, and learn from various sources. Where once I felt invisible in religious institutions, I now felt included and valued. Where once I felt limited by creeds and commands, I now felt empowered to make my life meaningful through practicing compassion, acceptance, and service.

Being a UU changed me, and Unitarian Universalism has continued to invite me to grow as a leader, an advocate for justice, and a participant in our church and in the world. I keep coming to UUCW today because I have found that church home I longed for. I am thriving in a community of loving, thoughtful people who celebrate life and value justice and human worth.

The questions that plagued my spirit before I came to UUCW have been answered so beautifully in this congregation of love and acceptance. I have found a freedom to form my own theology, which I call "the theology for the marginalized."

With the positive reinforcement I have received at UUCW, I've grown more assertive in standing up for my LGBTQ community and for my life. Where once I stood silently as gay jokes were told around me, or even laughed in an effort to fit in, I now speak up. Where once I cried when told to stay in the closet, now I am proud to love another woman.

When I came to UUCW, I didn't know much about environmental issues. I was here because I needed a church home where my wife and I could be welcomed and accepted. Although I believed in recycling and caring for our planet, I wanted to learn more. I've grown more aware by attending Earth Ministry films and presentations and by talking with members about global warming and other environmental issues. Just as I have felt like the other, so has our planet been the other for too long. My theology gained a new awareness as I added our planet to my list of the excluded ones I'm concerned about.

Through studying the Unitarian Universalist Principles, I've grown spiritually and come to value the following statements: There's no room for humor that puts down others, sarcasm that mocks people, and judgments that show contempt and intolerance. There's no place for apathy that ignores truth, fear that paralyzes action, and silence that enables inequality to flourish. Remaining quiet when hearing a prejudiced joke implies agreement with it.

I have always been a woman of faith, sometimes in Jesus, God, the Goddess, or Yahweh, and currently in Mystery, something greater within me (and others) and all around me. After spending years in religions based on creeds and dogmatic teachings, I feel free to seek truth and meaning in how I live and interact with others.

My theology for the marginalized has grown to include a statement by Parker Palmer in his book *Let Your Life Speak*. He writes, "Before you tell your life what you intend to do with it, listen for what it intends to do with you. Before you tell your life what truths and values you have decided to live up to, let your life tell you what truths you embody, what values you represent." Once I valued living according to ancient creeds and dogmatic decrees. I thought tradition was to be clung to as absolute truth. Now I follow my conscience to embrace justice fired by love and commitment.

Where once I feared being singled out as the other, I now live in my theology for the marginalized. Where once I felt crushed by prejudice and condemnation, I now realize we are all one. I see the hater and the hated as one, the shouter and the subdued as one, and the religious zealot and the spiritual humanist as one.

What began as my search for truth and meaning at UUCW has become a conviction that there is no "other," only all of us together in an interconnected circle of love and justice. At UUCW, I have gone from feeling excluded to feeling accepted and loved. What a life-changing journey! I've truly found my spiritual home!

The Spiritual Sense I Needed

Jack W. Rogers

The Church of the Larger Fellowship has been the strongest faith community I've had supporting me in my more than thirteen years of incarceration. I was a lay pastor in the Presbyterian church, but after my outrageous actions, I was totally cut off and abandoned by all members of the denomination and my local congregation.

In prison, I attended the Protestant services but found that the strong fundamentalist bent and the message gave me little spiritual fulfillment. When the prison invited a fire-breather who soundly told us that anyone who was gay was going straight to hell, I left and never returned.

Since college, I have always had the greatest respect for the Transcendentalists, especially Emerson, and I explored the Unitarian Church to find the spiritual sense I needed. I have always been a bit of an activist, and I admire the activism that has historically been a part of Unitarianism from the days of slavery onward through the segregation marches and the sanctuary churches. I feel at home in this group of spiritualists.

I have to admit to a bit of a depression in seeing what is happening in our nation with the hate and the rise of commercialism and putting profit over social justice. I see our nation entering into a dark period, and the only hope I see is for Unitarian Universalist congregations and others to march, seek social justice, and stand up for those who are going to be crushed in the name of profit.

I thank God for the long history of activism in Unitarian Universalist congregations, and I sincerely hope and pray that we are able to make a difference in the years to come.

Thank you for allowing those of us in prison to become a part of this denomination and sharing your efforts and the funds it takes to operate this extensive ministry. It means so much to all of us.

Why I Am a Unitarian Universalist

Leslie T. Grover

In the summer of 2016 I watched the city of Baton Rouge come to a boil over the death of Alton Sterling. I watched feelings run still higher and the city polarize even more with the deaths of three police officers less than two weeks later. I have made this city my home, but I have never belonged here.

There are some emotions that I can describe in words as I tell this story, but there are many others that I simply cannot.

If I died right now, as the song goes, I "wouldn't take nothing for my journey." I won't avoid naming the main character in my story: the Comite River. As I write this in late 2016, however, I cannot decide if the Comite is the hero or the villain of my story, because the tale is still dragging on.

The Comite River overflowed this summer, leading to flooding so bad that my son, my friend, and I all ended up trapped in the attic of my house, waiting for help for hours while we watched the waters swirl around us. Once we all got safely into a boat, my sense of the world changed. I don't really remember anything about that boat ride except the wind on my face as I passed through what used to be my nice, safe neighborhood. My insides felt stifled. Faces became blurred. I thought I heard someone sobbing softly, and after a while I realized it was me.

After a while the boat jerked, and one of the police officers on it said, "Ma'am, you can stand in the water now. But we have to leave you here to go get more people." And that was it. All of us disembarked into knee-high water, on our own in the middle of Lovett Road. We walked up Lovett toward a main artery of the highway. My friend and my son were far ahead of me, and as I waded my legs felt heavy, and I fell even further behind. Then an enormous F-350 truck pulled up beside us. The Confederate flag was prominently displayed, and a tobacco-chewing, Heart-of-Dixie-loving woman and her son stuck their necks out of the window. "You okay? Need a ride? Hop in!" she said. My son and friend came back to the truck. Meanwhile, the son of the woman in the truck abandoned his seat and got into the back. He held out his hand to my son, who took it and hopped into the back of the truck as well. My friend, who had been so calm and so strong during everything, climbed in, too.

I didn't respond to the woman's request at first. In fact, a fervent "no" rose up in the back of my throat, but it did not come out for some reason. Full disclosure: As a Black woman, I don't associate the Confederate flag symbol with helping people who look like me. In fact, I didn't initially think the lady was even talking to me. Several similar trucks were moving right past people searching for high ground to pick up stray animals. Some of the drivers carelessly splashed people as they drove into high waters, grabbing at dogs, cats, and even a small pig. So I thought she was talking to a dog that was trotting alongside us. But she was talking to me.

I took a running jump into the high front seat, right into mud and empty aluminum cans on the floor of the truck. I could smell the fresh pelts that were draped across the seat, right under the gun rack in the window. "Where do you want to go?" she asked. It occurred to me that I had no idea where I was going or even what I was doing. I looked out the back window through the rack. My son and my friend were talking to her son.

"Thank you, ma'am; please just take us as far away from this as you can." She nodded. We ended up at a gas station a few miles up, because the other roads in and out of the part of Central where we live were now flooded and closed. "God bless you," I told her, and I started to cry again. She smiled at me, and the young man helped me down out of the truck while he smiled, too. He was wearing a Confederate t-shirt with a deer head on it. We waved good-bye to them.

Eventually, after several hours in a local emergency shelter, we ended up at the home of one of my dearest friends, an emergency worker himself. That night I didn't sleep at all. I sat, and cried, and called the insurance company, trying to take control of a situation that no one could even begin to understand.

But the next morning, something happened that I did understand—phone calls. The members of my UU church started to call me. They offered me shelter, food, transportation, money, and even medical care. They reached out to me emotionally and spiritually, and when I went back to church, I was met by people crying, offering to help, and suffering with me. They did not lie to me and tell me everything was going to be all right. They did not say they understood if they did not. They did not tell me that everything happens for a reason. They just offered me their love, support, and presence.

The truth is, I have never belonged anywhere, not really. Though I came from a loving and supportive family, I was always "different." To this day, the way I see

life, the way I dress, the way I experience my humanness stick out like a sore thumb in most places and
among most people. When I was a child my inability
to fit in meant that I was sometimes treated with awe
and sometimes teased. As an adult, I get described with
words like "eccentric," "different," and "unusual." When
I went to church as a child, I felt protected. I knew that
no matter what problem or issue I experienced, I could
turn to God or my parents, or just pray, and it would be
okay. I really needed the church when I was growing up,
and I used to pray often to God to make me not stand
out. Instead I suffered through my awkward phases as I
grew up, with my past hurts often chipping away at my
self-esteem that was as fragile as choux pastry. And the
protections of childhood gave way to adulthood: disap-
pointments, abusive relationships, uncomfortable self-
actualizations, the deaths of childhood friends, illness, and
other difficulties that are not always easily understood.
The rose-colored glasses had been shattered, and the way
I saw ahead was not always positive, easy, or predictable.

Nothing captured the challenging parts of human
existence more than the summer of 2016 here in Baton
Rouge. This past summer was the worst one of my life.
Never have I felt so small and insignificant. This city has
great disparity between its citizens and perpetrates great
social injustices against its citizens of color. This summer

I witnessed Black lives being taken at every turn both by those in power and by those not in power, with hardly any recognition of their humanness. I saw the community here put out blue ribbons and hold fund-raising drives for the officers who were shot, and local businesses canonize them, without a word about the victims of racial profiling, hate crimes, or similar violence. I felt violated and invisible at the same time.

Then the flood happened, and I felt that nature in all her wrath, who ruined my home and could have killed me, my son, and my friend, did not see me as part of creation either. Never had I felt so much an outsider—politically, physically, and spiritually.

But the UU church and its members' responses of radical and immediate love changed that. I am the type of person who pays close attention to intuition—that feeling of energy like an innate "yes" or "no" in nearly all things. I look for a common energy in people, places, things, and experiences. The first time I attended this church, just over three years ago, I felt "yes." Now, as I recover from the flood and all the social trauma in this city, I often think back to that time. I remember how nice and welcoming the congregation was, but more than that, I remember feeling intellectually and spiritually at home during the services. While I am not exactly a social butterfly, after the service I found it easy to relax and talk with one or two people. I did not know it at the time, but that feeling was simply the energy of *agápe* love—a universal, unconditional love that transcends and serves. This summer, during the worst time of my life, that love took the lead. It saved me. It transformed me. It allowed me to belong.

At the UU church I am part of the fabric, and that fabric covers me as I grow spiritually and become the theologian that our youth minister sometimes talks about, while proceeding with the kindness our senior minister mentions so often. I now understand what it means to live in faith, because this church is about more than the church itself. It is about building up others, ourselves, and this community. I get to be Leslie, whoever she is, in all her iterations and with all her heart. I can shine out my heart and feel that love and acceptance shined back onto me from those sharing the church experience with me in a way that transcends race, gender, social standing, and even belief systems. For this type of love, I am grateful.

My Awakening

Karen J. McFarland

I jerked awake at 7 a.m. on a Saturday morning to the sound of my clock radio. A woman was speaking about the Return of the Goddess. I sat straight up in bed and listened in amazement. What she was saying not only resonated deeply within me, but started me on a journey that led to Unitarian Universalism.

The speaker, Charlene Spretnak, claimed that Western religion is inhabited only by male divine figures—Father, Son, and Holy Spirit or Ghost (also male, of course)—with women left out of the pantheon. I'm left out. But it wasn't always this way.

In ancient and prehistoric times, she pointed out, God was a woman! Societies of those times regarded women as all-powerful, since they alone gave birth to the entire human race, female and male, from their own bodies, and miraculously fed them from those same bodies. Males could not do this. Females also bled regularly, but did not die. Despite Freud's claims, the original envy was not "penis envy," but womb envy! Spretnak exclaimed, "The Goddess is alive and has returned!"

To say I was shocked is far too mild a description. And I was excited, too.

The year was 1982. The place was the small university town of Blacksburg, Virginia, where I was a freelance violist and music teacher. The radio show was "New Dimensions," from San Francisco, moderated by Michael Toms. And Charlene Spretnak was the editor of a new book titled *The Politics of Women's Spirituality: Essays on the Rise of Spiritual Power within the Feminist Movement*, an anthology of writings by feminist theologians, philosophers, activists, artists, poets, and deep thinkers. Before I even got out of bed, I determined to get this book and delve deeper into these intriguing new theories.

Our local independent bookstore didn't have it on the shelves, so I went to the city library. It wasn't there, either. I went to the university library. No luck. I was extremely frustrated but, deep down, not all that surprised. I finally mail-ordered it, and impatiently awaited its delivery.

When it arrived, I read it cover to cover, including all the footnotes and bibliography. There I read Mary Daly's critique of "God the Father," and shouted "Aha!" when she said that if God is male, then men are God.

I found Carol P. Christ's essay, "Why Women Need the Goddess," and her work on women's psyches. Chellis Glendinning, Hallie Iglehart, Starhawk (a practitioner of feminist witchcraft), Judith Plaskow, and Merlin Stone were some of those included in the book. My mind was blown open.

Blacksburg's independent bookstore did have on its shelves a surprisingly extensive selection of books on feminist theology, a new field of study. Clearly, there was another simpatico soul in this town! I bought all the titles the bookstore stocked and ordered many I found in the bibliography of Spretnak's book. I had a foggy memory of having seen some titles on my visit to the university library, so I returned there to find several volumes on feminist theology, including Starhawk's 1981 book, *The Spiral Dance*, about feminist witchcraft. Feminists were coming to theology later than to politics, art, or other professions. I took everything home. I couldn't get enough of these new ideas.

After finishing Spretnak's book, I realized her work could be considered post-Christian and I had been approaching the topic from the most radical viewpoint. I needed to see what mainstream Christian thinkers made of it. At the time, I was an Episcopalian, but I took myself to the office of the only female clergyperson in town, Catherine Snyder, a Presbyterian. I spoke of my dilemma and asked her if there were any writings by Christian women critiquing the male hierarchical system within the Christian religion. In retrospect I realize how radical it was for her to have these books on her shelves in the 1980s. Catherine warmly encouraged and supported me. She pointed me to the works of Mary Daly, Rosemary Radford Reuther, Elizabeth Dodson Grey, Carol P. Christ, and Elizabeth Schussler Fiorenza. I added these books to my ever-increasing library.

Once when I picked up several heavy texts at the bookstore, the young man behind the counter asked, "Are you writing a thesis?"

I bemusedly stuttered, "Noooo." I went away smiling to myself and thinking I could, or maybe even should.

After this beginning, I was on fire, talking about this subject to anyone who would listen. Fortuitously, Mary Carol Smith, a theological scholar, came to town and gave a talk at the university titled "The Importance of the Goddess." I convinced most of my friends to attend and we were the largest cohort of people there, by far. Smith confirmed all that I had been reading. A respected scholar of Sanskrit, she spoke of ancient history, anthropology, and archeological finds that supported her theory that goddesses had been the most powerful figures in the polytheistic pantheons of the ancient world. Her slides showed these ancient figures.

To learn more, I created a course in feminist theology for our local YMCA adult learning classes, designing it to learn more myself. I invited women I knew to teach one session each on a subject of their choosing. These folks included a professor of the New Testament at the local university, the Presbyterian minister I had first spoken with, a lay leader in the local Jewish congregation, and a professor from a nearby college whose specialty was philosophy and women. The course was a success. I organized a second one with different speakers. Out of this grew a group of women who continued meeting and discussing these subjects independently.

When my family moved from Virginia to the Upper Peninsula of Michigan in 1986, I continued my study of feminist theology and determined to dedicate my life to the service of women and girls. I had become convinced that, worldwide, women and girls are one of the most oppressed groups in modern history. Two years after that move, I took off for Boston to study with the premier feminist theologians of the time. I studied with Mary Daly at Boston College and marched on the president's house demanding her promotion to full professor, which was being withheld because her many books were considered "too popular, not scholarly reviewed." I studied with Elizabeth Schussler Fiorenza and Carter Heyward (one of the first women ordained a priest in the Episcopal Church), and heard Elizabeth Dodson Grey lecture many times. The years in Boston were inspiring, yet filled with many hazards and challenges as well.

Feminism is no guarantee against the intersection of oppressions that affect us all: sexism, racism, classism, homophobia, xenophobia. There was strife among us as we worked to understand the dynamics of oppression. I was scapegoated because I would not accept being labeled a racist white woman unwilling to work on her own prejudices. It was hard—and sometimes impossible —for many women of color to accept that some white women of good will were willing to betray their own privilege. The study of unacknowledged power is crucial to understanding the tyranny of human organizations. Power, I learned, is often more destructive when it is hidden. One has to go into the hall of power to dismantle hidden forces. It's like going into a labyrinth where the Minotaur waits to devour you.

When I returned to Houghton, Michigan, after two years in Boston, I knew that I could no longer squeeze myself into the narrow mold of Episcopalianism. The district bishop was unresponsive to my offers to assist in any way I could, even though I knew they were woefully understaffed and he had sent out a plea for lay help. A talk with the local priest convinced me he did not welcome my presence in his church. In the shadowy confines of a huge Richardsonian structure, I earnestly spoke with this man who was clearly threatened by the presence of a woman who knew the latest theological treatises and theories as well as or better than he did. I felt a great sense of relief walking out of there, knowing it was for the last time.

I thought I was far too radical to fit into any denomination or church again. In this tiny, windswept, snow-laden community, opportunities to engage in the work I longed to do seemed as remote as the Upper Peninsula itself. The only time in my life I've experienced a sense of panic was a day when I stood on the hill overlooking Houghton, bags of groceries clutched in my arms. As I surveyed this desolate place, I felt my stomach lurch. What was I going to do now?

My most liberal and progressive friends were members of the small local Unitarian Universalist fellowship, so I attended several times. When they learned I had been to seminary, they begged me to lead several Sunday services for them. At the time, the congregation was too small to have a settled minister of their own, so they were lay-led and always on the lookout for an interesting speaker. My first sermon was titled "The Return of the Goddess and Why It's Important for All of Us." It went over well. At the end, a man in the back of the room even stood up and suggested we sing the hymn "Turn

Back, O Man, Forswear Thy Foolish Ways." I laughed, but was relieved and humbled. I had found my people, my tribe.

After I had attended for several months and given more talks, someone said, "It's about time you thought about signing our membership book!" I did that in 1990, and have been a Unitarian Universalist ever since.

Gradually, I began to feel that my life's work was in the Unitarian Universalist ministry. I embraced the concepts of Unitarian Universalism: our seven Principles and six Sources. One of our greatest passions is the quest for social justice. Another is our commitment to saving the Earth and combating global climate change. My horizons had expanded beyond serving women and girls. I realized that everyone needs this healing message. I fondly say the Keewenaw UU Fellowship loved me into my ministry. They affirmed me as a strong spiritual leader.

As a UU minister, I have often had people tell me, "Finding Unitarian Universalism saved my life," or "It feels like coming home." I hear repeatedly, "I didn't think there was any place for me." This echoes what I felt when I became a Unitarian Universalist.

In times of great crisis such as the shootings at Sandy Hook, or natural disasters like tornados, my church opens its doors for silent prayer or healing and comforting rituals. My church steps up when people are hurting. I don't like to think where I would be without that cradling of support and human comfort.

As Starhawk puts it so well in her book *Dreaming the Dark*, "Community means strength that joins our strength to do the work that needs to be done. Arms to hold us when we falter. A circle of healing. A circle of friends. Some place where we can be free."

Unitarian Universalism offers the blessing of beloved community for me and countless others.

Unitarian Universalism has welcomed me home and affirmed my spiritual direction and choices. It has given me a circle of friends to hold me accountable—and to hold me when I falter.

The Mountain

Eric Bliss

It was a beginning like no other.

I was sixteen. It was my first Unitarian Universalist youth conference. Traveling winding valley roads and cliffside crags, we arrived at the Mountain an hour or so after dark—an actual mountain, owned and operated by Unitarian Universalists in the lush green canopies and smoky peaks of western North Carolina.

I stepped out of the cramped minivan, stretching my limbs, with the sounds of Simon and Garfunkel still reverberating in my psyche—on the tip of my tongue, like a snowflake.

Dear God, the stars. I've never seen so many. It was a crisp, clear February night, and they were so close, you could almost touch them. I tried, straining vainly in wonder, as a child might grasp for a toy just out of reach. Breathing in deeply, I felt an immense and overwhelming sense of peace and tranquility fill my being. I spun slowly, like a salt water taffy machine, the twinkling lights above me a blur.

Sounds of celebration broke my reverie, as laughter erupted from the meeting hall before me, glowing with light, broadcasting sounds of mirth and merriment.

I entered and was forever changed.

That night I couldn't sleep. My head was swimming. Full of smiles, and new faces. . . . A door had opened. A part of me, yet undiscovered, had opened.

I'm not sure of the hour, but it was very late. I crept down to the kitchen, as my throat was parched. Finding some hot cocoa, I bundled up with a blanket and shuffled quietly out, cupping my cocoa, onto the wooden porch of the lodge where we were staying, which extended out from the mountaintop, overlooking a darkened valley below.

I paused, sipping my beverage.

And the sun began to rise, silently yet triumphantly cresting the verdant mountaintops.

It felt like trumpets were playing in my soul. I was dumbfounded. Exhilarated. Humbled. Grateful. A speck in the universe. Alive.

"It's beautiful, isn't it?" an adult voice said from behind me. "Beyond description," I answered, breathless.

We stood in silence for long moments drinking in the sight, savoring it like sweet nectar from fresh honeysuckle.

And when I turned around, my mystery companion was gone.

Smiling, I returned to bed for a few ephemeral winks, eventually waking to the sounds of a discordant, untuned guitar attempting to play Aerosmith's "Dream On." Life can be funny.

Looking back, I know that I left a little piece of me on that mountaintop that brisk winter in North Carolina. But I also was reborn. Like the soap-white rhododendron blossoms that return each year, peppering that selfsame mountain in warmer months, and glistening with the perspiration of summer.

A Journey of Faith for Out Lesbians in the Deep South

Nan L. White

On Christmas Eve, 1995, I left the Presbyterian ministry, to which I had been called at the young age of sixteen. At the same time, Sam left a twenty-five-year career in the thoroughbred horse industry in Kentucky. We wept as we said goodbye to the place where we had first met, knowing we were choosing to end the careers that had led us to each other. Yet we were very excited to begin our life commitment as out lesbians. We traveled to New Mexico for education in our second career, massage therapy, hoping that we would be able to support ourselves financially. Nine months later, after completing massage therapy school, we landed in Beaufort, South Carolina, to set our roots in the soil of the rich Sea Islands, a land steeped in history and culture, and to which we were to discover an unexpected connection.

As we settled into Beaufort and our new life together, I was at a loss about what to do with my call to the ministry. I could no longer serve the Presbyterian church that christened, educated, and raised me, and had provided sanctuary for me in my youth. In 1991 I had become the first woman to be ordained by the Presbytery, but when I committed my life to Sam, the church rejected us both, no longer considering us worthy to continue serving as minister and ordained elder. We grieved deeply, but refused to go back into the closet. At one point, the Presbytery leadership did suggest to me that I "should just be discreet," but that was no longer an option.

Over time, my anger turned into depression. But the daily walks we took with our dogs on the sandy shores of St. Helena Island nurtured me.

Sam and I worked multiple jobs to pay our mortgage as we built our massage therapy practice; at one of these jobs I taught yoga at the YMCA. In 1999, after a morning class, a woman asked if I would help a group of people establish a Unitarian Universalist fellowship. Knowing very little about Unitarian Universalism, I asked her to tell me one thing UUs believe. And she answered, "We believe in the inherent worth and dignity of every person."

I replied, "Yes, ma'am, I'd be happy to help." Immediately I felt saved, knowing I could continue in ministry

—and in time I felt called to transfer my ordination and become a Unitarian Universalist minister.

My journey toward final fellowship with the UUA allowed me to explore theological questions I had had for many years but had never been encouraged to explore, not even in two seminaries and two internships —one in pastoral counseling and the other in clinical pastoral education. I ended up serving the new Beaufort fellowship for fifteen years, and they honored my ministry by awarding me the status of minister emerita in 2014. For six of those years I simultaneously served the Unitarian Fellowship of Hilton Head Island as a part-time minister. I created a Unitarian Universalist clergy cluster for ministers in the southernmost part of the UUA's Southeast District, which included North Carolina, and hosted a district meeting on the campus of Penn Center, where my office was located for eight years.

Penn Center grew out of the Penn School, which was founded by Laura Towne and Ellen Murray. They came to St. Helena Island in 1862 to found a school for formerly enslaved people newly freed by the capture of the Sea Islands by Union forces. Towne was a Unitarian, and it was her faith that drove her, together with the woman she loved, to dedicate forty years to the people of the island. Sam and I don't think we were as brave as Laura and Ellen, but like us they were women who loved each other and who journeyed to this place they did not know. The connection we feel to them is a powerful inspiration to us and often sustained me in ministry. Today, Penn Center serves as the center for Gullah history and culture on the Sea Islands. In my eight years there I helped create relationships between UUs and the Center that continue today. In particular, I built relationships with the Gullah people, who had first learned about Unitarians through Laura Towne 130 years earlier. The Gullah people's language, trades, and land are threatened by developers and our twenty-first-century values, and the Unitarian Universalist Fellowship of Beaufort worked together with them for justice. In 2011, the Penn Center inducted the UUFB into its prestigious 1862 Circle, which honors individuals and organizations that embody the Center's spirit and advocate for Sea Island history and culture. As its minister, I accepted the award on behalf of the fellowship.

My life, my ministry, and my ability to live openly with my wife as a lesbian couple are thanks to Unitarian Universalism. One woman asked me a simple question, and her answer to my question in response offered salvation to me, to Sam, and to my ministry. I am now in my twenty-fifth year of ordained ministry and serve a UU congregation in southern Oregon. As I approach retirement, my gratitude to Unitarian Universalism continues. Sam and I are deeply indebted to Unitarian Universalism for the freedom to live and serve as out lesbians.

Most of All, Mindfulness

Israel Luis Sanchez

About six years ago, I found myself in a prison administrative confinement, lost, confused, angry, and scared. Religion was a sour topic for me because it had no room for me due to my ideas and beliefs. There were those who claimed to share my views, but on occasions I'd see them dance to another tune. I felt alone, outnumbered, and defeated. Until the day I came across a copy of *Quest Monthly*. A small paragraph was underlined and the words I read were: "The enemy of religion is religion." Once these words caught my eye, I decided to read it from cover to cover. I discovered that the people behind this magazine might have a place they were willing to share with me. I contacted them and asked for more information. Thanks to them I've learned many things, but most of all, mindfulness. The Church of the Larger Fellowship has given me the tools so that I no longer feel lost or confused. I now feel it is okay to feel angry or scared sometimes.

With their help I've found the courage to get up and dust myself off and the wisdom that criticism can only knock me down if I allow it to. CLF, thank you so much for the push start.

Finding My People and Myself

Marie Luna

I didn't go to church regularly growing up. I would occasionally go to Catholic Mass with my grandparents, but I couldn't understand what they got out of it. To my child's mind, it seemed that they spent an hour a week in a place that they rarely mentioned outside of it. It was a confusing ritual of standing, sitting, and kneeling, and everyone kept their coats on, like they couldn't wait to leave. My most vivid memory is of being literally pushed away from the Communion plate by my grandpa. While I understand much more about this sacred ritual now, that was a big reason I didn't seek out church when I grew older. My limited experience of religion was mostly of being an outsider.

In 2003, my then-husband and I moved to Appleton, into a house that happened to be three blocks from a Unitarian Universalist fellowship. We drove by that building for over a year before someone mentioned that we should check it out. When I Googled the name, the Unitarian Universalist Association's website popped up. I vividly remember reading a message of support for gay marriage on the home page that day. I was quite shocked, as I had no idea that liberal religion even existed. I would never have expected to find a religion that fit my socially liberal values, or one that didn't require me to leave parts of me at the door.

After incredulously reading up on this brand-new-to-me religion, we walked over on the next Sunday. I remember little about the service, but I remember the energy. The warmth, the community of people who obviously liked each other and felt comfortable in that space. I remember the woman who greeted us with bubbling energy. I was home, and I hadn't even really met anyone yet.

Here are the people my age. Here are people I can look up to, people from whom I can learn how to age gracefully. Here are people to care for, who are younger than me. Here are small groups I can join to get to know others and myself on a deeper level. Here is the place where I learn just how big spirituality really is and the importance it has in my life. Here is where I can learn to name where I find meaning: exploring the Pagan faith, the Buddhist path, and pantheism. Here is where I make true, lifelong friends.

Here is where I learn what community is in all of its forms. Someone bringing me food that I can eat in the hospital, so that I can stay with my newborn son when he remains hospitalized for a month after he is born. Someone listening to me as I share my secret: that I need to get a divorce, but am terrified of doing it. The countless someones who were my cheerleaders and support system, and who loved me through all of my seemingly endless life transitions.

As congregational life coordinator at the Fox Valley Unitarian Universalist Fellowship, I have helped lead a lot of orientation classes. One of my favorite activities in them is sharing our spiritual journeys with each other. The first time I took the class, as a potential member who knew almost nothing about Unitarian Universalism and who had spent almost no time considering my own spirituality, I shared the high points (and a few low ones) of my life story. As others shared their true spiritual journeys, I started to see the difference. Being a member of the Fellowship has given me a new language to frame my life. I have been able to learn how I am a spiritual being and how my life has guided me toward spirituality in both small and big ways. I am grateful every day for what I have found within the Unitarian Universalist faith. My life has not just been changed in almost every way, but likely saved.

Saved by the Light

W. Garrett Jackson

I was drawn to Unitarian Universalism by the flaming chalice. Quite literally, I was saved by the light!

Growing up in Appalachia, I was surrounded by churches of all sizes and denominations. I was raised in a small, independent Protestant church, where if you didn't attend services on Sunday morning and evening, and on Wednesday evening, you weren't just not on the prayer list, you already had one foot through the gates of eternal damnation.

From a young age, I listened to weekly sermons that often disturbed me. Since they frequently degraded other denominations or faiths, I found myself wondering how that religion was supposed to be uplifting. Though the area wasn't known for diversity, there were Jews, Catholics, Mormons, even Amish, in our little community. Many of my friends at school were members of these "other" congregations and were some of the best people I knew. How was it that they were to be condemned to eternal flames because of their beliefs, or "non-belief," as I was being told? Why was dancing or wearing shorts so frowned upon? And just where did Cain's wife come from!?

I felt very depressed by religion. Something kept me from walking down the aisle to the altar to ask to be "saved," and that outward sign of inward change, known as baptism, was just not for me. I felt like a stranger in my own home and spiritual community because I questioned so much.

Looking back, I believe it was the internal divine spark that held me back. Or, perhaps it wasn't holding me back, it was just leading me down my own path, lighting my way. It wasn't that I believed less, it was that I believed there was more.

Most, if not all, of the churches in my hometown displayed a cross in some form on their structure or sign. While I attended a nearby college, I noticed a new church had entered our community, located just a few miles from campus. I thought it strange that a cross wasn't on the sign; instead, it simply displayed a flaming chalice. What was this Unitarian Universalism?

I began researching Unitarian Universalism as if I had to write a dissertation on it. Finally, after weeks of reading up on its history, famous people, and principles, I attended a service. I've never felt more at home and more moved by a spiritual community. There I was, sitting beside a Wiccan and across the room from a Native American, both of whom I had known in our community for years. The lay leader opened the service with a reading from an ancient Hindu text. Not only did it speak to me, but the smiling and nodding of heads throughout the room, even from the known atheist, spoke to me. Those words were from a specific religious faith, yet they were universal words. Words that spoke a truth to all who understood. This was definitely the place for me.

Unitarian Universalism has taught me more than just belief. The acceptance of being has been evident in each and every congregation I've interacted with. Lifestyle choices are not just acknowledged, they are celebrated, and people are accepted for who they are, which moves me spiritually. It makes me proud to be a human. To have this experience called life.

As I write this, I am incarcerated for mistakes I made in my professional life. I was ecstatic to find that Unitarian Universalism had a prison ministry so that I could continue to participate in my spiritual community. The correspondence from my home congregation and the prison ministry have satisfied my religious and spiritual needs. And not at the price of guilt or judgment. Acceptance and encouragement to rise above are instead the messages I have received.

The flaming chalice is more than just a symbol of our congregations. To me, it's a symbol of ourselves—the good works, kind words, compassion, and pursuit of knowledge that each of us is capable of, our individual piece of the divine spark. As a public servant, military service member, active citizen, educator, son, partner, father, and now as a prisoner, Unitarian Universalism has never made me feel the need to compromise my beliefs or sacrifice them. I can be who I am, what I am, and be accepted for all that I am.

A Gift to Me

Aisha Hauser

Unitarian Universalism was a gift to me. I have experienced this faith as a way I can be in the world without having to subscribe to the dictates of creeds I don't agree with. However, it has been difficult to be a Unitarian Universalist as a woman of color, one who wants the faith to live out the values it espouses.

I grew up in a fundamentalist home. It doesn't matter which faith—I've found that almost every person I've met who grew up with fundamentalist beliefs has had the same experience when it comes to the role of religion in family life. There is only one way, and deviating from that way will result in everlasting damnation. In college, I quickly turned away from such limited and destructive thinking. It wasn't until I had my own children that I sought out a new faith community.

I had already been to a UU service once, when I was twenty, at the Unitarian Universalist congregation in Summit, New Jersey. An intern minister was leading a spring solstice service by giving out tiny cloth bags of potpourri to symbolize the flowers and renewal of spring. I loved it, but had no desire to attend at the time. I was sick of religion, having just left my own, and didn't want to attach myself to a new one just yet. I did think, though, that if I ever decided to return to religion, it would be to the one that celebrated spring with bags of potpourri.

In the spring of 2003, my five-year-old daughter had a best friend who came from a family of conservative Christians. I didn't mind if my children spent time in their church—I thought I could get away with raising them with as "nones." However, as with sex education, if you don't teach your children, someone else will. Sure enough, my daughter came home from a Good Friday activity at their church and declared to her father, "Daddy, Jesus is the light of the world." My husband, who was not raised Christian, responded, "No he's not, we're Jewish." Since we weren't following any of the Jewish religious principles, I decided that I couldn't leave my children's religious upbringing to chance. Remembering the potpourri, I immediately looked up the closest UU congregation. I found one just ten minutes from my home.

We visited on Sunday, and when I asked the religious educator if they taught about hell, she answered, "Good Lord, no." As soon as she took the Lord's name in vain, I knew this was the place for me and my family.

I wasn't yet transformed—that happened when I took a class called "Evensong," led by the minister and attended by a varied group of members. It was a revelation for me to talk about my religious experiences and beliefs alongside others, some of whom held completely opposite beliefs. Some were atheists, one didn't believe Jesus existed at all, and I let them know that most days I am a theist, with some agnosticism thrown in on the days it was difficult to be on "Team God." I found a strange acceptance. I wasn't shamed or even challenged. Rather, the people would nod and say, *based on your experiences, it makes sense to me why you believe the way you do*. The fact that I could say I believe in God and the person across from me was an atheist and we could find common ground regardless was refreshing and gave me hope that religion could be positive and life affirming.

One unexpected part of my transformation as a Unitarian Universalist was an invitation to make peace with the religion of my upbringing. This didn't happen intentionally; in fact, the person who offered me the invitation has no idea to this day that she helped me become a better UU.

One day, an elder in the congregation asked me, "What did you like about being raised Muslim?" I answered, "Nothing. I didn't like anything and it wasn't positive." She looked at me steadily and said, "It couldn't have been all bad. You turned out fine, there must have been something good." I said I'd think about it. I pondered that question for a few days. And I found an answer.

I never internalized God as a man or even a person. I was raised believing that God is an energy and light that humans can't comprehend. This helped me to easily transition to our Unitarian idea of "one source." I was also taught about the value of sacrifice, which comes from Ramadan and the idea of voluntarily giving up food and water to reflect and more fully understand those who live in poverty. My mother instilled in me a deep sense of justice. No matter how little we had (we spent two years on welfare and food stamps), my mother always gave a tithe to remind us that someone else always has less and we always have to share.

When I thought about how the Muslim faith provided me with comfort and solace from the ideas that God is light and of the importance of sacrifice, I had a profound realization that I carry with me an important part of my childhood faith, while being a Unitarian Universalist. It is the pluralism of Unitarian Universalism that encourages my commitment to hold on to what is spiritually nurturing and let go of what is spiritually harmful.

Receiving and Giving

James Rogers

I joined the First Unitarian Universalist Church of Youngstown, Ohio (UUYO) in 1983, after being church-less for many years. As a child I had attended a black Baptist church, and then as a teen, a Pentecostal congregation. Neither of these church communities prepared me for what Unitarian Universalism has given me.

Before I discovered Unitarian Universalism, I saw religiosity as rigid, steeped in revelation and tradition that did little to help me grow and become a useful member of society. My immediate family, and everyone I grew up with, were comfortable with that rigidity. They questioned nothing and relied on revealed truths. What I heard from the ministers at UUYO was different. They confirmed my belief about how the world actually works and gave me the courage to express it to others. Unitarian Universalism welcomed me into a beloved community

—one that is not defined by a ZIP code but includes people all over the country, linked together by shared principles. I learned those principles at UUYO, and they were clarified for me when I attended my first UUA General Assembly (GA), in Fort Worth in 2005.

At that time Susan Frederick-Gray was my minister, and she asked me to be our congregation's delegate to GA that year. She even gave me money to help with registration and other expenses. Her only stipulation was that I write about my experiences there for the church newsletter. I remember feeling nervous and inadequate, because I had no experience writing for anything, but gamely participated in thought-provoking events and activities at GA and listened to wonderful stories of our progressive faith that is intent on doing the most good it can for as many people as possible. Just being around thousands of other UUs was exciting, and I enjoyed exchanging stories about our paths to this uncommon denomination. I also learned more about the origins of Unitarian Universalism. In the exhibit hall I bought a book edited by the late Forest Church titled *Separation of Church and State: Writings on a Fundamental Freedom by America's Founders*, which presented our country's history in a new light.

By going to GA I gained confidence, and in writing about it I discovered a gift for communicating; Susan's request kick-started my writing career. Since that first report for my church newsletter I have been published numerous times, and have worked as a contributing reporter for Examiner.com, an online publishing site. And I have attended five more GAs, most recently in Charlotte, North Carolina, in 2011. At each I've found books, met people, and had experiences that have enriched me, and my memories of them will last a lifetime.

I met Galen Guengerich there, senior minister at the influential and historic All Souls Unitarian Church in New York City—perhaps the most famous person I know! I've learned so much in his workshops, which I've attended at several GAs, taking so many notes you would have thought I was in college. He has introduced me to important historical authors, such as Voltaire, Milton, Shakespeare, and Aristotle, and to more contemporary ones, such as Paul Tillich. At GA in Minneapolis in 2010, I went up to him in a hotel dining room to show him something I had written down, and he told me I was onto something, and should keep taking notes. I keep in touch with him through email, and he even sent me an advance copy of his 2014 book, *God Revised: How Religion Must Evolve in a Scientific Age*, so I could review it for Examiner.com. One of his memorable comments remains in my notes: "We are at our best when in service to others."

My close friend Jack Brizzi, who died recently, was in service to others most of his life. We met at UUYO in the early 1990s and connected immediately. Like many others, Jack and I became UUs late in life, after experiences with faiths that didn't fit with the world as we understood it. Jack was my traveling companion for the six GAs I've attended, and he went to more than a dozen more without me. What I remember most about Jack is his interest in social justice, be it racial equality, gender equality, gay rights, or economic equality. These issues are in line with Unitarian Universalist principles and are often front and center at General Assembly. I will always remember returning with him from the 2008 GA in Ft. Lauderdale, when he suggested a side trip to Selma, Alabama, so he could revisit the places he had been to as a freedom rider in the civil rights struggles of the 1960s. In 2014 I watched the movie *Selma* with him, and we both paid special attention to the murder of UU minister James Reeb, which was a mobilizing moment in the struggle for racial justice. At the end of the film I noticed that Jack was tearing up, just as he had when we crossed the Edmund Pettis Bridge together six years before. Susan Frederick-Gray, Galen Guengerich, and Jack Brizzi, all Unitarian Universalists, have connected with me on a personal level, inspired me to accomplish important things, and enriched my life.

When Susan began her ministry at UUYO, Jack told me he had a hunch that she would one day become the first woman elected president of the UUA. In June of 2017 at General Assembly in New Orleans, that is exactly what happened.

I consider myself blessed to be associated with a people so bold.

I Only Have to Be Myself

Mark T. Vogt

If we are fortunate enough we touch and are touched by the hearts and souls of others—and are transformed. Transformation is seldom easy. It takes hard work, determination, perseverance, sacrifice, and often assistance from others. I do not know whether a complete transformation is possible, but I do know that I am not yet the man I wish to be.

I grew up in a household where secrets and problems were commonplace and silence the only commandment. I learned early on to keep my problems and fears to myself. I learned that punishment was more likely than sympathy or help. As a result, I have felt alone for much of my life. I have felt insignificant, unworthy, and incapable of doing anything to gain the acceptance of those around me, especially my father. I was arrested when I was twenty-two years old and I quickly learned what it really meant to be alone and to have no one to turn to.

After my arrest I donned a mask of indifference and told myself that I did not want friends and that I only wanted to do my time and go home. But in a world where hate was the norm, my kindness, generosity, and respect stood out. I developed friendships and the realization that I no longer wanted to be alone. I realized that I wanted and needed to change.

I stepped out of my comfort zone and challenged myself to interact with others. I enrolled in college and eventually earned a bachelor's degree in Behavioral Science. While I fed my mind, my soul starved. Though I no longer felt so alone I didn't feel like I belonged. Further change was necessary, and I slowly began to build a foundation of faith, spirituality, and belief.

I was a member of a Wiccan congregation at a New York correctional facility when I first wrote to the Covenant of Unitarian Universalist Pagans for a membership packet. I was expecting information and hopefully other resources that I could share with my fellow Wiccans.

Instead I received a message of hope and an invitation to join a community of acceptance and support. I discovered a faith and an organization of like-minded people who would accept me for the man I am today and not ostracize me for the man I used to be. I found a place where I could belong. I found a home and my soul sang for joy.

After reading about the seven Principles and the six Sources, I felt my own beliefs and ideals validated. I was amazed that I truly was not alone. Soon a small flame began to flicker deep within the recesses of my heart and soul and hope began to grow. Unitarian Universalism became a beacon of hope and light in the despair and darkness of prison, and I look forward to joining a congregation upon my release.

Unitarian Universalism has taught me that I am not alone in my struggle to become a better person and that there will be others there to support me when I fall short. I do not have to be perfect, beautiful, or smart. I only have to be myself. I do not have to be wealthy or popular to make a difference in the world. I only need to give what I can and to love my neighbor as I wish to be loved.

Most importantly, Unitarian Universalism has given me a community—a family—where I am valued, not for what I can offer but because I am me. I have learned that I am not insignificant and that I am worthy of love and respect. I can take on the world because I am not alone. As William Ernest Henley states in his poem "Invictus" —"I am the master of my fate, / I am the captain of my soul."

A Message of Peace and Hope

Eddee Daniel

One day in second grade, when some friends were talking about what churches they attended, my child Alex said, "Unitarian Universalist." When asked what Unitarian Universalists believe, Alex replied, "We believe in recycling!"

Our family has always loved that story, not just for its inherent humor, but for the underlying—if simplified —truths it contains. In a naive but precocious way, Alex expressed one of my own core beliefs about the cycle of life and death—that death is not the end of life but a transition that sustains the future. My second-grader also nailed the importance of action and personal responsibility within Unitarian Universalism. For me, church is about *doing* as well as believing. Our true beliefs are best revealed not in words but in how we live our lives.

How we were going to live our lives was at the forefront of the decision my wife and I made to join a Unitarian Universalist church. Little did we know at the time how profoundly that decision would affect us. The original impetus was momentous enough: literally a matter of life and death.

In 1991, the United States had declared war on Iraq and I found myself on the street outside the Federal Building in downtown Milwaukee with a crowd of protesters. Although I was no stranger to anti-war protests—I came of age during the Vietnam War era—I realized that this time I no longer had a church home or a community of like-minded people for support. The need for such support was driven home forcefully when a student in the high school at which I taught threatened me with bodily harm for my anti-war stance.

As a youth I had had the kind of community that I now realized I missed. I had been raised in a very liberal and activist Presbyterian congregation in suburban New York. The minister was my father, who put his own life and faith on the line for the civil rights and anti–Vietnam War movements. But for various reasons my Christian faith had been sorely shaken during my college years at the University of Wisconsin–Madison. I had become distant, literally and figuratively, from both my religion and my father. I had successfully suppressed their absence until the onset of the Gulf War.

I was despondent. I felt that I needed a faith community, because I couldn't face that despondency alone. I needed to gather with others in support and solidarity. Although my wife, Lynn, had been raised in a very different home environment, she was similarly affected by the war.

It was at this moment of fragility and need that friends invited us to attend a Christmas Eve service at Unitarian Universalist Church West (UUCW) in Brookfield, Wisconsin. Although unfamiliar with Unitarian Universalism at the time, we attended and found a message of peace and hope that for me was particularly resonant. It felt like coming home. On that fateful night we found the nurturing community we were seeking. Twenty-five years later, long after the troops returned home from that brief war, we are still members. Our lives have been changed in too many was to enumerate.

With only a small dollop of hyperbole, Lynn likes to credit our church with saving our marriage. Unlike me, she was distrustful of organized religion and did not feel an immediate connection, no matter how welcoming the congregation. Raised as an atheist, she did not have the kind of positive image of churchgoing that I did. Although initially she felt the same need for a supportive community, she was skeptical that a church could provide it. At the time our children were two and four years old and she also didn't share the urgency I had begun to feel to provide them with a religious component to their upbringing.

UUCW surprised her. The non-creedal, non-judgmental atmosphere was a revelation. Sermons that emphasized personal responsibility and active participation in social justice issues stood in stark contrast to her previous understandings of religion. She was relieved to find a place where people were not punished if their beliefs and convictions fell outside religious and social norms, where atheists were not only tolerated but welcomed, and where no one was trying to convert her to their own version of spirituality.

Our respective families were equally appalled at our decision to become Unitarian Universalists, but for opposite reasons. My Presbyterian parents assumed I'd fallen from grace, while Lynn's atheistic parents were alarmed to learn that she had "found religion." The warmth of the congregation and our newfound understanding of Unitarian Universalism's inclusivity made the transition less stressful. Not only was our marriage strengthened by our new relationship to the church, but in time both of our families came to respect our decision when they realized that we had not been lost to them.

Lynn's initial resistance to subjecting our children to the "indoctrinating" influences of Sunday school was so thoroughly overcome that she ended up volunteering to teach religious education herself. We both wanted our children to be raised with the good news that Unitarian Universalism had to offer: that all of life is beautiful and valued, that we are all interconnected, that not only is it possible to effect positive change in society but we have the responsibility to work to make it happen. While we both welcomed the new foundation that UUCW provided us as individuals and as parents, the effect on our children was even greater.

Alex's insight in second grade was the beginning of a life of activism and continual transformation for him—he went on to become a UU spiritual activist and religious professional. Alex, who identifies as queer, transgender, and radical, explains that he never had to "come out" because there was never a closet in his UU upbringing. This is a source of pride for me as a parent, but also a testament to the accepting and nurturing environment that Unitarian Universalism provided.

My daughter Chelsea was also inspired by her UU upbringing in ways that changed her life. One of the most important ways that our church engages in its stated mission of "building a better world" is a biannual service brigade in Nicaragua. Her first such experience, during her high school years, inspired Chelsea to major in Spanish and social work in college. Then, upon graduation, she returned to Nicaragua for an internship, where she met her future husband. She is now a bilingual social worker in Milwaukee.

Sadly, war has remained a factor in our family's relationship to our spiritual community. The short Gulf War that was so pivotal in our initial awakening to Unitarian Universalism has become a seemingly never-ending conflict. Our UU faith and the UUCW community continue to sustain us. As Lynn recently reflected, "Last summer Alex, now an adult, described his faith to me. He views Unitarian Universalism as nothing less than the liberal faith that *can and will* transform the negative effects of the kind of religious fundamentalism that harbors fear and war. We are furthermore *called* by our faith to be agents of change. Where did he get these ideas but through our church?"

Lynn, who had no religious home when she was growing up, was particularly struck by the fact that their own church home has given both Alex and Chelsea their personal paths to transform the world. As for us, knowing as we do now that our children would benefit so clearly from their UU upbringing would have been sufficient reason to be part of this vital denomination. But we too have been transformed. Twenty-five years of

Unitarian Universalism have given us hope in the face of fear, courage when despair threatens, and peace in a world full of conflict.

What Church Says That?!

Donald Ernest Allee

For so many years, I can't say how many exactly, I felt disconnected from any church or community as a whole. It was such a left-out feeling that suicide crossed my mind several times.

So imagine how I felt, two and a half years ago, alone, in prison, after already serving more than twenty years, with more than twenty-five more left to go. I was living in a housing unit with about a hundred guys, all of us alone, lonely, and hurting inside. The only things we have to help alleviate our sufferings are each other—the ways we can devise to keep from going insane or becoming militant—and things we can read.

As luck would have it, on a bookshelf in one of the housing units here at Two Rivers Correctional Institution lay a magazine with a fascinating cover . . . *UU World*. As I began to flip the first pages and saw words, it was like water to a dying man in a desert; my eyes nearly began to tear up. Words like justice, truth, liberty. What church preaches this!? What the heck? They accept outcasts, even LGBTQs and atheists!?

I had never found a "church" like this in more than fifty years—never knew it existed. I saw a list of famous people who were all members of Unitarian Universalist churches at one time. "Wow!" I said in amazement. "This is what I've been looking for!" I wrote to them, as soon as my pen found paper. What did I find? In time, I learned that the church has its issues. For example, there are not enough people truly involved to help maintain contact with others who have recently joined. And, yes, they don't have time to address every prisoner's social injustice on an individual basis. But, they are on the frontlines and in the battle trenches fighting for our rights even if it is in public protests, wanting real changes, not bullshit, not just trying to loot and/or get your picture taken so someday you'll be a part of a history book on the era!

And then, history is made. And there they are, victorious, right in the thick of the battles.

I wrote to them, and they were accepting of me. Graciously, they gave. I began taking their "New UU Correspondence Courses," replying with my own voice on paper. And I heard other voices, just like mine, those of prisoners. And I could identify with nearly every one of them.

Issue after issue of *UU World* came to me, freely, each month. I read nearly every article of every issue. (And that of the Church of the Larger Fellowship's monthly *Quest*.) Cover to cover. And I liked what I found. A lot! It felt like . . . home. It talked about beauty, love, and words that we mere humans can understand, in our caveperson "great mystery" instead of "God"—that white-bearded white man floating on a cloud, just waiting to damn you to hell if you don't do as you're told. A second life, after you've screwed this one up. Fairy tales. All done up, with pomp and dogma, threats and illusion. Unbelievable stuff.

And then there is this church that tells you, "If you need someone to tell you what to believe this is probably not the church you should attend." What church says that!?

My church, that's what. A church that truly does something—besides sit around and collect tithe money! A church that actually tries to promote peace and harmony, respect, love, and the enforcement of rights!

Has the Unitarian Universalist's view of life changed my life? Absolutely, it has. It helped me see beyond the fantasy. What's truly important? What we do today. How we treat each other—in *this* life. We could be kinder to each other, a lot kinder than we are. But, there are those—so hurt—all they can do is lash out at the world. And they are the ones who truly *are* in hell.

Notes in the Margins

James C. Key

Scanning the books of Papa's library, I couldn't help but notice the copious marginal notes in his prized book collections: the complete works of Shakespeare, American and English writers and poets, Latin and Greek texts, and more than a few King James versions of the Holy Bible. These scribbles often noted his suggestions for rewording for clarity, references to related texts and sources, and, not infrequently, disagreement with what the authors had to say. Many notes reflected his wry humor. As a bookworm in the public and school libraries, I knew better than to mark any book in any way. Even schoolbooks in the early grades could not be marked, as they were on loan and had to be returned clean for the next class to use, or the offender would face a hefty fine. So it was shocking to an eight-year-old to notice these penciled notes in the fine books I knew my grandfather cherished.

Papa lived in North Carolina, and his eldest daughter, my mother, lived in Virginia about a hundred miles away. She was a single mother of five. After many extended absences, her husband, my father, had abandoned the family permanently before my birth. During school holidays, Mother would often take me on the Greyhound to see Mama and Papa and some of her eleven brothers and sisters whenever she hit a bad patch. My siblings were much older and seldom made those trips. So it was during those visits in my early years that I began to explore Papa's library—with his permission, of course. He tried to hide some of the more lurid *True Detective* magazines to which he subscribed, but I inevitably found them and was fascinated by those marginal notes as well—very educational for a young lad.

During those many visits, I was invisible to most of my uncles and aunts and older cousins. However, Papa was pleased with my curiosity and took an interest in my theological education. Over time, I came to realize that although he identified as a Social Gospel Methodist and was an enthusiastic advocate for the social justice element of that movement, he was highly critical of the Gospel element as he saw it being preached and practiced in the Jim Crow South.

He was a member of a large Methodist Episcopal Church South congregation and received the minister's visits with enthusiasm. They spoke regularly and with great intensity, with Papa challenging the theological justifications of church-supported segregation and other errors of theology he observed. He was highly critical of the absence of any prophetic voice by white clergy on the immorality of this social construct.

These conversations—debates, really—were most informative for an inquisitive child who was always eavesdropping. They always left me with questions that my Methodist catechism teacher was unable to answer: Why would a benevolent God condemn people to hell? Why would a loving God not allow certain types of people into heaven? How could you reasonably explain three gods in one? It just didn't make sense to me.

And those notes in the margins always intrigued me! On every visit I found an excuse to browse Papa's library to look for and try to understand his marginal musings. They provided great insight into his self-education in Latin and Greek, with particular emphasis on translations of the Gospels in the Christian Bible.

On one of those visits, I was browsing an old, worn, zippered Bible when my eyes stopped at a bold inscription in the margin of one of the Gospels: "Bull Shit!" I laughed loudly, which alerted Papa to my snooping. It launched a long conversation between a curious kid and a delighted-to-influence grandfather. He explained the importance of reason as I matured and developed my own understanding of God and the universe. He told me about the Jefferson Bible, the document that Thomas Jefferson created to clarify Jesus' teachings to provide "the most sublime and benevolent code of morals which has ever been offered to man." Jefferson omitted anything that was "contrary to reason," deleting anything that could not be supported or verified. Papa introduced me to Jefferson's deism and the notion of a benign "watchmaker" divinity.

Throughout that visit, he valued my doubts and welcomed my questions. Months later, my mother and I moved to North Carolina to live with my grandparents for what turned out to be two years. That move initiated a two-year tutelage by my grandfather in the application of reason to all things I found curious. The experience set the stage for my early embrace of Universalism and, later, Unitarianism, in belief if not in membership. I remained active in liberal Protestantism as I grew older, married, and started a family, all the while a cultural Christian and moving toward a belief I would ultimately identify as religious Humanism.

Like the proverbial frog in the hot oil, I tolerated my increasing discomfort with the theology of liberal Protestant communities as I moved the family around the United States. Living and working in Asia increased my interactions with people of different cultures and with different theological and philosophical worldviews.

After living all over the United States and Asia, I moved to a small town in coastal South Carolina and was finally introduced to Unitarian Universalism . . . by a Presbyterian minister! The minister thought I would be welcomed by some folks who were organizing an emerging Unitarian Universalist congregation. She was right. The frog had become uncomfortable enough in the hot oil to jump out and become a part of a religious community that welcomed doubt, reason, science, and intuition more than certainty.

Not long after joining this Unitarian Universalist community, I was diagnosed with stage IV non-small-cell lung cancer and prescribed a palliative course of chemotherapy that ultimately lasted ten months. The prognosis was grim: Mortality rates were 95 percent within one year and 99 percent within five years.

In hindsight, I realize I moved through the five stages of grief quickly. I sped through denial. I had, after all, smoked as an adolescent. But I quickly entered the angry stage. I had quit smoking more than thirty-three years before the diagnosis and had eaten properly, exercised regularly, and seen my health-care providers as suggested. I shouldn't be facing this diagnosis! I have no recollection of the bargaining stage. As a religious

Humanist, I believed that my recovery was entirely dependent on the effectiveness of the available science, my own positive attitude, and the visualization techniques I had been introduced to at Duke University Hospital. So there was no bargaining and also no depression, the fourth stage of grief. As I reached acceptance, it became clear to me that it was precisely my emergent Humanist belief that equipped me to face what then seemed like a death sentence.

There was no deity to blame or petition for a cure, no miracle to hope for. There was, however, a revelation, if you will, that this newly acknowledged Humanist outlook liberated me so that I could choose a path that put me in control of my treatment and recovery. It was this belief system that led to healing.

My realization that Humanism was a healing point of view led me to look back at the financially strapped, single-parent household I had grown up in. Despite the hard times, frequent bean dinners, many moves, and rude questions from adults, I never felt that our situation was my fault. It wasn't some sin, original or recent, that had led to our lifestyle. Nor was it because of some God that someone had made angry. Papa's insistence on applying reason to all challenges—spiritual, moral, and ethical—gave me the insights that led me to Humanism: first to my Universalist views that rejected the notions of sin and hell, and then to my Humanist views within Unitarianism that embraced the rational and the inherent worth and dignity of humankind.

As I researched the disease, consulted with medical professionals, underwent treatment, and relied on the support of my faith community, I became increasingly convinced that human energy and understanding would get me through the nightmare. Great science from a world-class medical university, compassionate care from a legion of health-care professionals, a loving embrace from my faith community, and a positive outlook of hope all contributed to a full recovery. Fifteen years on, I am in excellent health.

I believe that my commitment to religious Humanism within Unitarian Universalism saved my life. I had a grandfather who encouraged me to examine all things good and bad through a lens of reason, including reading, study, and research, considering alternatives and honoring intuition. I had a community of heretics who supported me with compassion, encouraged my approach to restoring health, and never judged. And I had a family who were there at every step and never suggested I needed to get right with any divine. All of this and more continues to affirm and strengthen my identity as a religious Humanist.

To our great sadness, Jim's cancer recurred after he wrote this piece, and he drew his final breath on June 2, 2017. The love and devotion that he gave to Unitarian Universalism lives on and we feel his spirit with us still.

—Meg Riley

From the Cellblock to Seminary

Eli Poore

It's sometime around 11 p.m., and I'm lying in a prison cell in Gatesville, Texas, staring at the cement ceiling and listening as cell doors slam and chains and keys rattle in the distance. Somewhere, further down the hall lined with individual cells, someone is singing what sounds like a hymn, and its echoes reverberate softly off of the walls of my cell. Even though it's after "lights out," it's not completely dark; the gray-green glow of fluorescent lights from down the hall streams in, illuminating the graffiti scrawled on one of my walls, and from the outside, the exterior lights pour their orange glare in through my window. I was transferred from another unit earlier that day and was amazed to discover that I could actually open my window—I'd spent months in a place where I could not even see outside. So I did just that; I cranked it open excitedly and let the crisp fall breeze blow through. Having that little bit of control over my environment and access to the outdoors, even through a barred window, feels a little bit like freedom, the most I've had in many months. Lying in my bed, I feel that breeze again, blowing gently across my face. It chills me a little, but I don't care, and I pull my blanket up, adjusting my head to a cozier position on the state-issued jacket that I've been using as a pillow since arriving at the prison in July. I listen to the night noise outside: crickets, and an owl somewhere in the distance. I close my eyes and try to shut out the light and all of the other sounds, and I lie there still, listening, in the dark.

For the past several months I've been doing my best to cope with another kind of darkness entirely, one that creeps into my thoughts and dreams, wakes me from sleep, keeps me restless and unsettled even during the brightest parts of the day. I believe that each of us is capable both of doing immense harm and of assuaging it, and the ways I've hurt others, as well as the ways I've been hurt, weigh on my mind. It used to be easy to stifle these feelings; all it took was a little money, exchanged for some painkillers or a little heroin, and they vanished. All my tortured anguish dissolved as the opiate euphoria spread throughout my body, numbing, comforting. Lying here in my cell, I have no such escape, and few distractions from the tumult of shadows that swirl in my head: people I've loved, places I've been, things I've done or didn't do, my pain, fear, and regret all traced out in dizzying trails of smoke and ink.

I've always loved the nighttime. When I was a child I would go outside, reveling in the quiet and still that settled just after twilight, when the stars started to appear, one by one, and the moon illuminated the trees and houses and cars with an otherworldly, lucent silver-blue. Night is different in prison, however: still quiet, but in an almost eerie way. Our thoughts naturally wander before we drift off to sleep, and it's the same here in prison, only the air seems to echo and thicken with a thousand thoughts and memories, rife with shame and regret, denial, violence, attrition, self-reproach. Each night I've added mine to the chorus, sometimes stifling the sobs that rise wildly in my chest, sometimes not, all the while knowing that, ultimately, the only way out of my own darkness is through it. I've fought for months, pushing back those shadow figures, those memories of hurt I've experienced, and, most painfully, hurt that I've caused.

Tonight, though, it's different. I hear the crickets outside. The air, grown frigid, creeps in through my open window and I shiver, burying my head beneath the blanket. I take a deep breath and move forward, into the black. My world wrenches and twists, my lungs heave, and my eyes are burning with tears. The sky outside has turned from black to cobalt in the east, and it will be morning soon. I don't know how long I've been crying.

It's a sunny sort of Saturday five years later, and I'm cleaning out a drawer in my bedroom that has accumulated a large collection of random stuff, as drawers in my house are wont to do. Among the junk mail, scribbled notes to the kids reminding them to take out the trash, old birthday cards, and batteries of uncertain status, I come across a worn blue notebook, and my heart flutters a bit. Several years ago, I scrawled "Ephemera" across the front of it, intending it for notes about this and that, small writings, nothing of real significance or importance. But it became something much more relevant—and uncomfortable.

I begin flipping through it. The first few pages are indeed random jottings, but after that the journal entries begin. I read a few lines, rifle through to the back, read a few more. At that point, the feelings flood in again, and I have to close the notebook.

I began writing while I was incarcerated, not long after that night that I broke down, overcome by guilt, shame, and regret for the things I had done and the things that had been done to me. Every thought, every regret, every hurt, every painful memory and shameful secret was spelled out in that notebook in gritty detail. I wrote for months. Things I had never talked about or shared with anyone were all set down there, shadows that now stare back at me in the sunlight. Though I've mostly made peace with them, I'm overwhelmed by the memory of how unbelievably painful it was to finally acknowledge and accept them. For a moment I sit there, eyes closed, reminding myself that things are different now. I breathe deeply, bringing myself back to the present moment, reconnecting with my spiritual center. For many years I thought I had lost it, but in the end I learned that it was just obscured. Looking back, I know that I began reconnecting with it on that cold night in my cell. It blew in gently, like the breeze that drifted through my open window and over my face, as I began to come to terms with what I had done. That night I stepped into my own darkness and was stunned and overcome by it. It was an essential step in my process of healing and, ultimately, redemption.

The story of how I came to be in the cell that night is complicated. It began in a doctor's office when I was around eleven or twelve years old. I was prescribed hydrocodone for migraine headaches and a slew of sports-related injuries. Such a prescription was not uncommon in those days. I still recall feeling the opiate warmth settle on me for the first time. More ominously, I recall thinking how nice it would be if I could feel that way all the time.

Growing up in the conservative Texas Panhandle, I became a spiritual seeker at a young age. My first connection with Unitarian Universalism was with the Amarillo Unitarian Universalist Fellowship. The community enlivened and emboldened me in exploring alternatives to the fundamentalist theology that was so prevalent in both my immediate family and the community. I drew strength and encouragement from like-minded adults and youth who were drawn to Paganism, Buddhist philosophy, Humanism, and myriad other sources of wisdom and ritual, and to the Unitarian Universalist tradition of inclusion, social action, and progressivism. Also, as a queer, gender-fluid youth, I felt empowered by the acceptance I received from the church community. One Sunday I saw a pamphlet about Unitarian Universalism and the queer community, and as I scanned it, I was struck by the phrase "the worth and dignity of every person." What a contrast to the pervasive judgment, bias, and "love the sinner, hate the sin" rhetoric that I had experienced from members of other denominations! They denigrated my self-worth and made me feel that I was wrong, evil, or of less worth than others because of who I loved. These years saw the height of the religious right and the Moral Majority, and a political climate that gave voice to people like Jerry Falwell and James Dobson. And yet here was this church with a rainbow-emblazoned pamphlet. This was a different kind of church, indeed.

For most of my school years, I was an exceptional student. I was promoted a year in elementary school and again in high school; I took the SATs at fourteen, scored in the 99th percentile, and began college a few months after my sixteenth birthday. I loved music, art, poetry, and literature, and was a veritable bookworm. I was especially attracted to the controversial and seditious: writers like William S. Burroughs, musicians like Kurt Cobain, artists like Jean-Michel Basquiat. The themes of their work stood in contrast to the repressive, conservative values that I found pervasive in my community and in the world at large, and I was drawn to the "tortured artist" archetypes that they embodied. I found something oddly glamorous and romantic about unappreciated and tormented genius.

After graduating from high school, I began experimenting more and more with drugs, oscillating between periods of abstinence and times when I indulged in everything from prescription drugs to cocaine. One by one I was losing my connections to the community that had brought me such sustenance. Eventually I was using painkillers regularly, moving on from Vicodin to Percocet and eventually OxyContin, and suffering chills, yawning, muscle cramps, and insomnia whenever I stopped. I knew that these were symptoms of physical dependence. I was still in college, and my grades suffered. I dropped classes, or stopped going altogether. And when OxyContin became too expensive I tried heroin. Immediately I became an IV user.

The year 2005 was a turning point for me. In August I lost my father, who had struggled for a long time with depression and illness, to suicide. I was devastated. I cut off contact with my family and friends and binged on every drug available, overcome by my grief and not caring at that point if I lived or died myself. His loss pushed me further on my downward spiral. As I fell deeper into my addiction, I dropped out of college. One by one I lost jobs, family members, and friends. I lost every piece of myself that I valued, including my spiritual life. I went from associating with casual users to spending my time with hardcore addicts and criminals, thieves, dealers, and traffickers. I bounced between jails and rehab programs, and spent some time on methadone maintenance.

I received my first two felony convictions, for possession of methadone and for using a family friend's credit card without permission. I had bought gift cards with it, to trade for drugs. My mother encouraged her to press charges, trying to get me sent to court-ordered rehab. Ultimately, I turned down a probation period in favor of a six-month state jail sentence, knowing that I had no intention of stopping using and would never be able to successfully complete the probation period. Sure enough, I was using heroin again within twenty-four hours of my release.

Eight months later, I found myself spiritually bereft and both emotionally and physically ravaged. I had used my mom's credit card without permission, again to buy gift cards to trade for drugs, and just as she had urged her friend to do earlier, she was pressing charges. Still, she gave me the option of taking responsibility for the credit card bill and going to rehab again, and although our relationship was understandably rocky, she let me stay with her at her place in the country for a few days. Although I was not a theist and did not believe in any sort of interventionist deity, one night I sat beneath the stars on her back porch, saying a silent, desperate prayer for healing, knowing that I had reached the end. I could take no more.

The next morning, four sheriff's deputies came and arrested me on three outstanding warrants: two for the charges my mom had filed, the third an enhanced shoplifting charge. I recall feeling a sense of relief at my arrest, hoping that perhaps this could really all be over. In the back of the police car on my way to jail I felt a sort of eerie peace; as I watched the trees go by, still bare and brown from the winter chill, I had a sense that perhaps my life would change, perhaps this time I could really be done, and I felt a glimmer of gratitude for the possibility.

I spent about three months in the county jail before I was called to go to court. After working with my court-appointed attorney, I agreed to accept a plea bargain of two sentences of four years and one of fifteen months, to be served concurrently. There was no offer to go to rehab instead. I felt numb as I went before the judge and signed the papers, going through the motions almost mindlessly. I had the opportunity to hug my family one more time before being taken away to a holding cell in the basement of the courthouse, where I wept, alone and in chains, feeling lost, destitute, and emotionally wrecked, not knowing when I would be able to see my family again, and in disbelief that my life could have taken such a turn. I was the one everyone had been sure would make it, the one who would become a doctor, an attorney, or a classical pianist. After all, none of us plans on becoming an addict or a felon.

It took a little more than a month for me to be

transferred to the Texas Department of Criminal Justice women's intake facility in Gatesville, Texas, and from there I was transferred to the nearby Christina Melton Crain Unit. It was there that I had my first breakdown—or breakthrough, as the case may be—and began processing all that had happened in the past few years. As well as making journal entries, I wrote letters, slowly reconnecting with family members who had all but given up on me. My correspondence with my grandmother, in particular, became a regular source of inspiration and strength. She encouraged me, sent pictures, told me stories, said that she believed in me and wanted to see me succeed. Hearing my name at mail call was a reminder that someone in the world was thinking of me; it was a lifeline that many of my fellow prisoners did not have.

Little by little, I began to heal. I began meditating again. I found a book in the library that I had read earlier but found particular meaning in now: *Peace Is Every Step*, by Thich Nhat Hanh, in which he describes the power of mindfulness. For a while I worked on the Field Squad, a modern-day version of the chain gang. We walked out to the fields every morning at 6 a.m., accompanied by guards on horseback with rifles, and were made to cut grass, among other things. We also planted vegetables, and I found a connection to the earth there, despite the desolate and oppressive surroundings. One particular day we were planting potatoes, and I did a breathing meditation as I hoed the rows . . . swing, swing, breathe in, swing, swing, breathe out. I began finding little bits of peace despite the oppressive system in which I found myself. I began meditating regularly, doing yoga in my cell, writing, reading, making art, and slowly healing.

On July 4, I watched the fireworks in the distance through the bars of the day room in my maximum security prison unit, and two days later I was released on parole, reunited with my family. I was incarcerated for nearly eighteen months.

After my release, I made arrangements to attend a faith-based recovery center in San Antonio, Texas, which had connections to the United Methodist Church. The staff, counselors, and administrators were wonderful and understood that my beliefs differed from those of my housemates and those in the program material. They made accommodations for me, only asking that I be respectful and participate fully. I was required to attend a religious service of my choice at least once per week, and I chose to visit the Shambhala Meditation Center regularly, which was easier to get to by bus than the Unitarian Universalist church in San Antonio. I also enjoyed several services at Travis Park United Methodist Church downtown, which was a progressive, socially active congregation.

After completing the program, I moved to Corpus Christi, Texas, with my new partner—someone whom I had met while incarcerated. We were looking for a fresh start and found it among the palm trees and ocean breezes on the Texas Gulf Coast.

When we arrived in Corpus Christi we knew no one, with the exception of a few co-workers. But, informed by my experiences with Unitarian Universalism as a teenager, I knew where to find like-minded people, and I searched for a Unitarian Universalist church or fellowship in Corpus Christi. My partner and I visited the Unitarian Universalist Church of Corpus Christi for the first time, and were welcomed by people who became our church family. Both of us are musically inclined—my partner is a singer and I am a guitarist, pianist, and bass player—and we connected with the band leader and were invited to sit in on a practice session of the church's house band, Thoreau Rocks. We jumped in, played and sang together, and were welcomed with open arms. We were invited to coffee by two band members who have become friends and mentors, encouraging us, inviting us to functions and events within the community, and generally keeping us involved. Our two children, conceived before we met each other, joined our new family, and they have been involved in the children's religious education program and are now part of the teen group.

We participated in social justice activities, my partner joined the board, and I became a lay leader and Worship Committee member. We shared our stories with our community members, and they shared theirs with us. In their eyes we were not criminals or miscreants, but instead two of their number, "wanderers, worshippers, lovers of leaving." We were welcomed into community, loved, included, our worth validated and our dignity honored.

My involvement with and connection to my church community for the past six years has been a process of healing as well as a dance of mutual spiritual growth and discernment. We laugh together, love together, share joys, triumphs, and grief. The power of this community and of my experiences has created within me a deep desire to be of service to others, to connect with others on a spiritual level, to work for justice, to dismantle systems that denigrate and marginalize communities, to stand against anything that denies the worth and dignity of every person, to work for peace and justice, to promote compassion and understanding. Indeed, I feel that this desire has been with me all along—and recently it has been transformed into a calling to ministry. I want to connect with others and engage together in spiritual exploration and expansion, upholding the Principles of our faith tradition, bearing prophetic witness, and creating beloved community. I went through a period of discernment, and at last applied to, and was accepted into, the Master of Divinity program at Starr King School for the Ministry, where I will seek fellowship and ordination as a Unitarian Universalist minister. I began my studies in fall 2016 and hope to graduate in 2019.

My path has been a winding one, but these days I am overwhelmed with gratitude. I have been transformed by our faith, and I seek to be, together with my faith community, a vehicle for the transformation of others. I have witnessed firsthand the systemic oppression that exists within the criminal justice system, and I recognize that I experienced it from a place of privilege as a white, middle-class person. Still, as a gender-fluid, queer-identified person, I can be fired for my sexual orientation without repercussions. For me, dismantling the systems that deny the worth and dignity of any person is a theological task, and one to which we all are called by the tenets of our faith. We have much to do as a people of faith, but I believe in the power of community, compassion, love, gratitude, faith, and justice—power that is represented by and within our tradition. May we all be transformed, redeemed, healed, blessed, and renewed by one another, and may we bring those blessings to others throughout our communities through conversation, compassion, and commitment. My life is but one of many that have been transformed by our Unitarian Universalist faith, and I look forward to seeing our legacy continue, and to being a part of our movement as a Unitarian Universalist minister. Though I have some obstacles to overcome in that process as a result of my past, I have faith in the forgiveness of our community and draw strength and encouragement from those within it.

Together We Know Freedom

Nathan C. Walker

My parents had a vision—to transform forty acres of desert in northern Nevada into a lush alfalfa farm. They could not do it alone, so they solicited all the help they could get, including from me, their eldest son. I was eight years old when I drove a beat-up Ford pickup while my dad stood in the truck bed and threw fence posts into the drought-stricken sand. We cultivated the soil and constructed huge pipes on wheels to spread the water from one side of the farm to the other and back again. Eventually the dream came true: the forty acres of desert were transformed into a lush sea of green. I was taught early that it is possible to reap what you sow, a metaphor found in many sacred texts.

Although my folks were not religious, they were devotional. Many Sundays we went horseback riding in the Sierra Nevadas. I never explicitly asked them, but always suspected they were the founders of the Equestrian religion. After setting up camp, we would sit around the fire and tell stories. My mom and brother would pull out their guitars and we'd sing songs; my dad would recite poetry; we'd sit in silence and make wishes upon falling stars, surrounded by the beauty of Lake Tahoe. The material, the tangible, the natural became a catalyst for our reflections on the non-material aspects of life.

But there came a time when not even nature could address social questions. When I was fifteen, my dad found a love letter in my pants pocket written to . . . my boyfriend. It was 1991. I had started my first year of high school, where my classmates were preoccupied with the rodeo and where their trucks were armed with gun racks. In response to my coming out, my grandmother grabbed my hand and said, "I hear there's a lesbian up at the Unitarian fellowship." And off we went to meet the lesbian.

I have a confession to make: I don't remember ever actually meeting the lesbian. I do remember that this little fellowship of a dozen people met in a trailer in Reno, Nevada. I found something remarkable that day: community. It was a community of people who renounced fanaticism. They proclaimed reason. They promoted religious freedom and cultivated humanity. And the Unitarian Universalist Fellowship of Northern Nevada is now over two hundred members strong; they have built a sanctuary next to that trailer.

I am aware that this small gaggle of Unitarian Universalists—including a lesbian—was built on content developed by the Church of the Larger Fellowship. I remember asking, "What's a 'church in a box'?" We'd open the materials the CLF sent us and a man would read. It was so simple: we sat around a chalice, told stories, sang songs, sat in silence, and expressed our hopes and dreams. I look back on those simple exchanges and wonder if this small group of people felt like they were planting seeds in a drought-stricken land. Little did they know what they would reap: how the very act of planting the fellowship saved my life. Literally.

In my nightstand lay a knife, a note, and a calendar. I was counting down the days until I would take my own life. Unbeknownst to my grandmother, there were only two days left on the countdown on that fateful Sunday morning. A small group gathered and provided for me an oasis in the desert of despair. I was hungry for belonging and they fed me hospitality. I was thirsty for self-worth and they offered me a cup of acceptance. I was a stranger and they welcomed me. Together, we knew freedom.

At that time, the Church of the Larger Fellowship was aware that printed material was the most efficient way to disseminate the saving message of Unitarian Universalism. The founders of this local fellowship knew that the most accessible place to advertise their location was—you might remember this—the phone book. So my grandmother used the Yellow Pages to find their address. She gave me a folded map, and we drove nearly an hour to gather in fellowship.

Today, the CLF is exploring innovative methods to serve dispersed people throughout the globe. Think for a moment about the kinds of tools we now have at our disposal to achieve this goal. Look back on how technology has changed in the last ten years, and imagine what's to come in the next ten years.

When I was eight years old, the neighboring farms all shared one party phone-line, and therefore my technological training consisted of mastering the art of lifting the telephone receiver without the other people on the line realizing I was eavesdropping. I am a part of the last generation who learned how to type on a typewriter; the last generation who sent handwritten letters to a pen pal; the last generation who listened to 8-tracks and cassette tapes, who rented movies from stores and watched them on VCRs, who wrote checks.

Today, eight-year-olds are learning to read and type by sending text messages; they have video pals across the world and use translation software to communicate; they eavesdrop by setting their iPod Touch to record while they leave the room, giggling. Today, we are trained to download music and movies, to instantly get everything we want, and to swipe cards rather than exchange green paper. When we want to get directions, we use our phones to show us the most efficient route according to a global positioning system, and when we reach our destination we broadcast our arrival to the world. Our world is changing, and change is inevitable. But what else is change? Could it be an invitation for us to transform?

I'm reminded of the words of Huston Smith, a scholar of comparative religions, who said, "The century's [technological] advances must be matched by comparable advances in human relations."

This is the primary question that the CLF is now poised to ask: How will we use technology to cultivate humanity? How will we use the tools of our time to be the religion of our time? How will we reach those wandering in the deserts of despair? How will we overcome the boundaries of time and place to achieve things we could not do otherwise?

Take, for instance, a love story: the story of a bride and groom whose mothers were ill and unable to attend their wedding. This couple gathered with a few friends in the historic chapel of the First Unitarian Church of Philadelphia. With a laptop we Skyped in one mother from the Ukraine and the other from Los Angeles. From around the curve of the world the mothers witnessed the wedding from their hospital beds. After the ceremony we cuddled around the laptop screens to take a photo of the uniting families. Thanks to technology, we were able to achieve something that would otherwise have been impossible.

And so, for the members of the great Church of the Larger Fellowship, the quest has begun. What stakes will they make? How will they collectively master the art of being a religion of our time and the art of being human? They may keep using technology effectively, but continue to remember that it's not about the gadgets—it's about connecting, it's about creating opportunities for intimacy, it's about cultivating humanity. In an age of technological advancements, there must be comparable advances in human relations.

All we have to do is create a safe place, whether real or virtual, where people can gather: where people are known, where they know they matter, where they know they belong. All it takes is an invitation to gather, and something magical will happen. When they gather, our living tradition will teach them how to, as Maya Angelou says, mold their dream into the shape of their most private needs and sculpt it into the image of their most public selves.

They will do so when they gather in trailers, at kitchen tables, in Internet cafes and prison cells. They will do this whether they are online or off to serve our country. Let us never forget that no matter how fast technology may evolve, one thing will always remain constant: people will gather. They will gather, time and time again, to celebrate, to mourn, to tell stories, to sing songs, to sit in silence, and to make meaning of their lives.

And as the CLF continues to serve dispersed people throughout the globe, the people will continue to come. Soon enough, some grandmother from some remote corner of the world will come and ask its senior minister, the Reverend Meg Riley, "Are you the lesbian of the larger fellowship?"

In that remarkable moment, something important will become clear: that grandmother is not alone. At her side is a child—a child who has long since mastered the art of despair. And Reverend Meg will reach out, kindle a flame, tell stories, sit in silence, and cast a thousand wishes into the sunrise. Together, they'll look out onto the lush landscape that was once a drought-stricken desert to bask in abundance. And together they will know freedom.

To find a Unitarian Universalist congregation
near you, visit uua.org.

To learn more about
The Church of the Larger Fellowship,
a Unitarian Universalist congregation without walls,
visit clfuu.org.